A BIBLI(
POINT OF VIEW ON
INTELLIGENT DESIGN

KERBY ANDERSON

HARVEST HOUSE PUBLISHERS

EUGENE, OREGON

Cover by Dugan Design Group, Bloomington, Minnesota

Cover Photo © Michael Simpson / Taxi / Getty Images

INTELLIGENT DESIGN
Copyright © 2008 by Kerby Anderson
Published by Harvest House Publishers
Eugene, Oregon 97402
www.harvesthousepublishers.com

Library of Congress Cataloging-in-Publication Data
    Anderson, J. Kerby.
    Intelligent design / Kerby Anderson.
        p. cm.
    Includes bibliographical references.
    ISBN-13: 978-0-7369-2291-3
    ISBN-10: 0-7369-2291-1
    1. Intelligent design (Teleology) 2. Evolution (Biology) 3. Religion and science. I. Title.
    BS651.A56 2008
    231.7'652—dc22

                                                                    2008002116

Printed in the United States of America

        08 09 10 11 12 13 14 15 16 / VP-SK / 12 11 10 9 8 7 6 5 4 3 2 1

Contents

THE CONTROVERSY

WHERE DID WE COME FROM? Why are the earth, the sun, and the universe here? How did life arise on this planet? These are fundamental philosophical questions with great scientific implications. The current theory of origins states that life arose on this planet by chance and that all of the cosmos is the result of a material cause.

But does the scientific evidence support this? Evolutionists say that it does, but there are other views that certainly challenge this fundamental assumption. Some of those who challenge Darwinian evolution embrace the idea of intelligent design. These include scientists, teachers, and even politicians.

The visceral reaction to the idea of intelligent design can be seen in many articles, editorials, op-ed columns, and blogs. One of the more significant recent incidents came in 2005 when President George W. Bush held a lighthearted conversation in the White House with representatives of Texas newspapers. Knight Ridder's Ron Hutcheson asked about President Bush's personal view concerning the idea of intelligent design.

After some joking back and forth, President Bush ventured, "That decision should be made to local school districts," but he felt that "both sides ought to be properly taught." Hutcheson followed up with another question, and President Bush responded, "I think that part of education is to expose people to different schools of thought, and I'm not suggesting—you're asking me whether or not people ought to be exposed to different ideas, and the answer is yes."[1]

Bush's answer set off a firestorm and a monthlong debate that included a *Time* magazine cover titled "Evolution Wars." The cover art featured a parody treatment of the Sistine Chapel, showing the bearded figure of God with His arm outstretched and His finger about to touch a chimpanzee. The subtitle read, "The push to teach intelligent design raised a question: does God have a place in science class?"[2]

The question to President Bush and the subsequent debate goes back to 2004, when a school board in Dover, Pennsylvania required biology teachers to read a one-minute statement concerning intelligent design. By the end of 2005, those school board members were voted out of office, and a U.S. District Court ruled in *Kitzmiller v. Dover* that the required statement was unconstitutional (a topic we will address more in chapter 9).

It is also worth noting that President Bush wasn't the only politician to address the topic of intelligent design. Senator John McCain (R-AZ) told the *Arizona Daily Star* that he believed intelligent design should be taught in schools. "I think there has to be all points of view presented. But they've got to be thoroughly presented." He added, "There's nothing wrong with teaching different schools of thought."[3]

During a Republican presidential debate in 2007, the candidates were asked whether they believed in evolution. Senator Sam Brownback (R-KS), Mike Huckabee (former governor of Arkansas), and Representative Tom Tancredo (R-CO) indicated that they did not.[4] Senator McCain said that decisions about what is taught should be up to the local school districts. The controversy surrounding these statements led Senator Brownback to write an op-ed piece for *The New York Times* to further explain his position.[5]

In order to understand the nature of this controversy, we need to look at what journalists and scientists are saying about this idea of intelligent design. And we need to look at how proponents of intelligent design have been responding to these criticisms.

What do critics say about intelligent design?

Some critics say that intelligent design is nothing more than religion. Consider this comment that appeared in the Sunday Book Review section of the *Los Angeles Times:* "The problem is not its underlying theology—a matter properly left to individual religious belief—but its disingenuous masquerade as a form of legitimate scientific inquiry."[6]

The author essentially has a twofold criticism. First, the author takes a shot at religion, implying that it is a matter of personal preference, not truth (a topic we will explore in chapter 2). Second, the author also takes a shot at intelligent design by saying that it is simply religion masquerading as science (a topic we will discuss in chapter 8). Essentially he is saying that intelligent design is not only religious, it is deceptive.

The author goes on to say that it is also void of any substance: "In the border war between science and faith, the doctrine of 'intelligent design' is a sly subterfuge—a marzipan confection of an idea presented in the shape of something more substantial."[7] In other words, intelligent design is not only a subtle attack on science, but it offers nothing more than a hollow pastry of evidence.

Of course similar arguments have been made about the theory of evolution. In fact, it is ironic that the article writer used the metaphor of a dessert, which parallels a comment made a few years earlier by University of Massachusetts Amherst biologist Lynn Margulis concerning the theory of evolution. She said, "Like a sugary snack that temporarily satisfies our appetite but deprives us of more nutritious foods, neo-Darwinism sates intellectual curiosity with abstractions bereft of actual details—whether metabolic, biochemical, ecological, or of natural history."[8]

Many critics argue that intelligent design is not science. John Roach, writing for *National Geographic News,* asks the question, Does intelligent design threaten the definition of science? He believes that "intelligent design theory may change the very definition of science by allowing the supernatural into the lab."[9]

Other critics believe it is more than just a redefinition of science. They see it as a frontal assault on science that is doing great harm to scientific research. One editorial in the journal *Cell* put it this way:

> The attack on Darwinism by supporters of Intelligent Design is a straightforward attack on science itself. Intelligent Design is not science because it proposes a supernatural designer as an explanation for evolutionary change. It is quite extraordinary that the Scopes trial of the 1920s is once again being revisited in parts of the US where attempts are being made to replace scientific teaching in schools with explanations based on religious beliefs.[10]

What is at stake in the origins debate?

While there are many who regard the debate about origins as peripheral and inconsequential, most of the critics of intelligent design see it as a crucial debate.

One well-known critic of intelligent design is professor Kenneth Miller at Brown University. When Miller spoke at Hamilton University in 2006, a reporter gave this account of his talk:

"Why is this a big deal?" asked Miller. The answer, according to Miller, is the future of science in America. We are raising a generation of people who are going to be suspicious of science, and that has huge implications for scientific fields. Other countries will be moving ahead in science, leaving the United States behind. "What is at stake is, literally, everything," said Miller.[11]

Gerry Wheeler, executive director of the National Science Teachers Association, agrees. He believes that the promotion of intelligent design is hurting science education in America: "It sends a signal to other countries because they're rushing to gain scientific and technological leadership while we're getting distracted with a pseudoscience issue."[12]

Critics believe that a major reason the United States is lagging behind other nations in science education is due to the promotion of creationism and intelligent design. And they believe that proper science education will make students better citizens and enable them to make wise choices in the political arena concerning candidates and issues. Therefore, they reject teaching alternative theories of origins.

Oxford University biologist Richard Dawkins recently acknowledged, "*Even if there were no actual evidence* in favor of the Darwinian theory…we would still be justified in preferring it over rival theories."[13] That is a remarkable statement. Even if there weren't evidence for evolution, he is so committed to it that he believes scientists should prefer it over any other alternative theory of origins (especially over intelligent design).

Another professor made an even more incredible statement. He said, "Even if all the data point to an intelligent designer, such an hypothesis is excluded from science because it is not naturalistic."[14] In other words, even if the evidence points to intelligent design rather than to evolution, it is excluded from consideration because it is not based upon the worldview of naturalism.

Isn't it ironic that scientists who uphold the value of the scientific method and pursue scientific research would have such disregard for the scientific evidence itself? After all, it is this evidence that enables scientists to arrive at their scientific conclusions about the world around us. Unfortunately, many scientists are willing to ignore evidence that does not conform to their prior assumptions and worldview.

In the next chapter, we will look at the connection between evolution, naturalism, and Darwinism.[15]

DARWINISM AND NATURALISM

MOST WOULD AGREE THAT the intelligent design movement grew out of a criticism of the philosophical basis of evolutionary theory. Professor Phillip E. Johnson, a law professor at the University of California, Berkeley, began the discussion with his first book, *Darwin on Trial.*[1] In it he examined the scientific evidence for evolution and its philosophical basis. His second book, *Reason in the Balance,* examined the influence of the philosophy of naturalism in the spheres of science, law, and education.[2] And his third book, *Defeating Darwinism,* brought his case to high school and college students.[3]

Now what prompted a law professor to start writing about evolution? It turns out that while on sabbatical, Johnson began reading books on evolution. He noticed that when evolutionists wrote for the general public, they presented the *fact* of evolution and implied that the important elements regarding evolution were settled. But when they wrote and talked among themselves, they admitted that there was still no consensus about how evolution occurred. When I was in graduate school over 30 years ago, I noticed that same phenomenon. The public discussion of evolution was very different from the private, in-house discussion.

Johnson argued that many evolutionists held to the theory not so much because of a preponderance of scientific evidence, but because of a commitment to the philosophy of naturalism. *Naturalism* is the belief that everything that exists is a result of natural or material causes.

By definition, naturalism excludes the possibility of intelligent design because of the assumption that only natural causes can be studied by science. Because Darwinian evolution is the best naturalistic theory for explaining origins, scientists willingly assume that it must be true.

What is the relationship between science and religion?

In order to make sense of the world, many people today accept the idea that truth can be found in two realms. Nancy Pearcey writes about this in her book *Total Truth*.[4] She says that our society has divided truth into two categories, which she calls the sacred/secular split or the private/public split or the fact/value split. They are different ways of saying the same thing. Religion and moral values are subjective and shoved into the upper story, where private opinions and values reside. And in the lower story are hard, verifiable facts and scientific knowledge.

Darwinists accept this split and have even tried to convince Christians that in this way religion is safe from the claims and conclusions of Darwinian evolution. But a brief glance at the books that appear on the best-seller list shows that evolutionists regularly invade this upper story of values with their harsh criticism.

In *The God Delusion,* Richard Dawkins says that religious belief is psychotic and arguments for the existence of God are nonsense. Sam Harris echoes that sentiment in *Letter to a Christian Nation.* Daniel Dennett, in his book *Breaking the Spell,* believes that religion must be subjected to scientific evaluation.

In her book, Pearcey shows that Darwinism leads to naturalism.

She says that "Darwinism functions as the scientific support for an overarching naturalistic worldview."[5] And this is a naturalistic view of knowledge where "theological dogmas and philosophical absolutes were at worst totally fraudulent and at best merely symbolic of deep human aspirations."[6] In other words, if Darwinian evolution is true, then religion and philosophical absolutes are not true. Truth, honesty, integrity, and morality are not true but actually fraudulent concepts and ideas. If we hold to them at all, they were merely symbolic but not really true in any sense.

Daniel Dennett, in his book *Darwin's Dangerous Idea,* says that Darwinism is a "universal acid." This is his allusion to a children's riddle about an acid that is so corrosive that it eats through everything including the flask that holds it. In other words, Darwinism is too corrosive to be contained. It eats through every academic field of study and destroys ethics, morality, truth, and absolutes. When it is finished, Darwinism "eats through just about every traditional concept and leaves in its wake a revolutionized worldview."[7] In a moment we will come back to the impact evolution, naturalism, and Darwinism have had on religion.

How did naturalism become the dominant philosophy?

Today, scientists usually assume that scientific investigation requires naturalism. But that was not always the case. When the scientific revolution began (and for the next 300 years), science and Christianity were considered to be compatible with one another. In fact, most scientists had some form of Christian faith, and they perceived the world of diversity and complexity through a theistic framework. As we will discuss in chapter 8, many of these scientists (such as Copernicus, Bacon, Galileo, and Newton) tried to understand the world as a creation of God and therefore developed scientific tools and methods to explore and understand it.

By the nineteenth century, secular trends began to change the perspective of scientists. This culminated with the publication of *On the Origin of Species* by Charles Darwin. His theory of evolution provided the foundation needed by naturalism to explain the world without God.

Darwin believed that natural selection, rather than divine creation, could account for the origin of all living things. He wrote in his autobiography that the argument for design in nature "fails, now that the law of natural selection has been discovered." He added, "There seems to be now more design in the variability of organic beings and in the action of natural selection, than in the course which the wind blows. Everything in nature is the result of fixed laws."[8]

In many ways, Darwin was reacting to a particular view of creation, which assumed that all species were individually created by God. In his writing he describes his opponents as holding that each variety of finch on the Galapagos Islands was created in that state by the Creator. He rejected the idea that the unusual flora and fauna were "created in the Galapagos Archipelago, and nowhere else."[9] He also rejected the idea that these were all among the innumerable acts of creation.

Charles Darwin therefore rejected the idea that all of life was intelligently designed. He wrote to Sir John Herschel:

> One cannot look at this Universe with all living productions & man without believing that all has been intelligently designed; yet when I look to each individual organism, I can see no evidence of this. For, I am not prepared to admit that God designed the feathers in the tail of the rock-pigeon to vary in a highly peculiar manner in order that man might select such variations & make a Fan-tail.[10]

By the twentieth century, G.K. Chesterton was warning that

Darwinian evolution and naturalism were becoming the dominant "creed" in education and the other public arenas of Western culture. He said it "began with Evolution and has ended in Eugenics." Ultimately, it "is really our established Church."[11]

No longer was a Creator necessary. Natural selection (and later the addition of information about mutation) provided the necessary pillars for a naturalistic foundation. As one evolutionist put it: "By coupling undirected purposeless variation to the blind, uncaring process of natural selection, Darwin made theological or spiritual explanation of the life processes superfluous."[12]

Today, it is easy to see how scientists believe that naturalism and science are essentially the same thing. They often slip from physics to metaphysics, leaving the boundaries of science to make philosophical statements about the nature of the universe. While scientists can tell us how the universe operates, they cannot tell us if there is anything outside of the universe.

But that didn't stop astronomer Carl Sagan in the PBS program "Cosmos." The first words he utters are, "The cosmos is all that is or ever was or ever will be."[13] In other words, the universe (or cosmos) is all there is: no God, no heaven.

Notice that Carl Sagan's comment is not a scientific statement. Rather, it's a philosophical statement. And it set the ground rules for the rest of the program. Nature is all there is. In many ways, Sagan's words sound like a creed. It is as if he were attempting to modify the Gloria Patri: "As it was in the beginning, is now and ever shall be."

So influential are these ideas that they can even end up in our children's books. Author Nancy Pearcey tells the story of picking up a science book for her son, *The Berenstain Bears' Nature Guide*, which featured the Berenstain bear family. The family goes on a nature walk, and a few pages into the book appears a sunrise with the following exclamation, including the capital letters:

"Nature…is all that IS, or WAS, or EVER WILL BE!"[14] Sounds like a heavy dose of Carl Sagan's naturalism packaged for young children, doesn't it?

How does naturalism influence science today?

Naturalism is the framework scientists use today in their work. For example, a physicist at Case Western Reserve University wrote a letter to *Physics Today* and contended that science must rest upon the philosophy of naturalism. He argued, "The first criterion is that any scientific theory must be naturalistic."[15] He and other scientists are essentially arguing that unless the theory is naturalistic, it must be excluded from consideration. So by definition, they exclude the concept of intelligent design.

The editor in chief of *Scientific American* stated that "a central tenet of modern science is methodological naturalism—it seeks to explain the universe purely in terms of observed or testable natural mechanisms."[16]

Tom Bethell, writing in *First Things,* pointed out how ingrained this philosophy has become in science. He says that anyone who believes in naturalism "must, as a matter of logical necessity, also believe in evolution. It is accepted simply because it is the only alternative. No digging for fossils, no test tubes or microscopes, no further experiments are needed." Naturalists accept evolution because of their philosophical commitment to naturalism. Tom Bethell concludes: "He knows that is true, not because he sees it in the genes, or in the lab, or in the fossils, but because it is embedded in his philosophy."[17]

Evolutionist Richard Lewontin made a candid admission regarding this. "It's not that the methods and institutions of science somehow compel us to accept a material explanation," he admitted. "On the contrary, we are forced by our a priori adherence to material causes to create an apparatus of investigation and a set of concepts that produce material explanations." He therefore warns that this materialistic philosophy must be "absolute, for we cannot allow a divine foot in the door."[18]

Have naturalism and Darwinism become a religion?

Phillip E. Johnson, in a chapter titled "Darwinist Religion," points out that a belief in evolution is often loaded with religious and philosophical implications.[19] Darwinian evolution rests upon the philosophical foundation of naturalism. This means that the evolutionary process proceeds through random processes. The evolutionary process has no goal or purpose.

The U.S. National Academy of Science attempted to address this question in a 1981 resolution that said, "Religion and science are separate and mutually exclusive realms of human thought whose presentation in the same context leads to misunderstanding of both scientific theory and religious belief." Essentially this was an attempt to appeal to the fact/value split discussed earlier in this chapter. In other words, evolution is a fact in the real world, and religion is a faith commitment in another world.

Paleontologist Stephen Jay Gould even argued that among evolutionary biologists there is "an entire spectrum of religious attitudes—from devout daily prayer and worship to resolute atheism." Phillip E. Johnson noted, however, that he has found "a great deal more of the latter than the former."[20] After speaking on college campuses for more than 30 years, I have come to the same conclusion.

In many ways, Darwinism has become a substitute religion. Some scientists have been candid enough to argue that they believe that the teaching of evolution will actually put an end to any religious belief. Astronomer Steven Weinberg says, "I personally feel that the teaching of modern science is corrosive to religious belief, and I'm all for that!" He adds that this hope is "one of the things that in fact has driven me in my life." And if science can bring an end to religion, "it would be the most important contribution science could make."[21]

This should not be surprising, because that was the impact the theory of evolution began to have in the nineteenth century. Julian Huxley observed that "Darwinism removed the whole idea of God as the Creator…from the sphere of rational discussion." He added, "Darwin pointed out that no supernatural designer was needed; since natural selection could account for any new form of life, there is no room for a supernatural agency in its evolution."[22]

"Evolution by natural selection, for instance, which Charles Darwin originally conceived as a great theory, has lately come to function more as an antitheory, called upon to cover up embarrassing experimental shortcomings and legitimize findings that are at best questionable and at worst not even wrong. Your protein defies the laws of mass action? Evolution did it! Your complicated mess of chemical reactions turns into a chicken? Evolution! The human brain works on logical principles no computer can emulate? Evolution is the cause!"[23]

—**Robert Laughlin,** Nobel laureate physicist, Stanford University

---

British scientist John Randall points out, "There can be little doubt that the rise of Darwinism played an important part in undermining Victorian religious beliefs."[24] And J.W. Burrow concedes that perhaps more than any other work, Darwin's book shook man's belief in "the immediate providential superintendence of human affairs."[25]

Evolutionists have been honest enough to admit that Darwinian evolution serves as a sort of religion to those who hold to a naturalistic view of life. Michael Ruse says, "Evolution came into being as a kind of secular ideology, an explicit substitute for Christianity," he notes. And it "is promulgated as an ideology, a secular religion—a full-fledged alternative to Christianity, with meaning and morality." So he must admit that "evolution is a religion. This was true of evolution in the beginning, and it is true of evolution still today."[26]

In his book *Reason in the Balance*, Phillip E. Johnson agrees: "What has really happened is that a new established religious philosophy has replaced the old one. Like the old philosophy, the new one is tolerant only up to a point, specifically, the point where its own right to rule the public square is threatened."[27] A theistic worldview has been replaced by a naturalistic worldview not only in science, but as Johnson shows, also in such disciplines as law and education.

What is the significance of humans in an evolutionary worldview?

Leading evolutionists have, for decades, addressed the question of human significance. If evolution is a random process, then how significant are human beings? Paleontologist George Gaylord Simpson wrote, "Man is the result of a purposeless and natural process that did not have him in mind."[28] Stephen Jay Gould wrote that evolution has knocked human beings off their pedestal because "*Homo sapiens* is but a tiny, late-arising twig on life's enormously arborescent bush—a small bud that would almost surely not appear a second time if we could replant the bush from seed and let it grow again."[29]

Today a group of scientists and philosophers known as the New Atheists drive home the same point. Daniel Dennett says, "In the beginning, there were no reasons; there were only causes. Nothing had a purpose, nothing has so much as a function; there was no teleology in the world at all."[30]

"Primate studies is based on a simple principle: Humans share 99 percent of our genes with the chimpanzee, and therefore the 100 percent chimpanzee can help us understand ourselves...we share perhaps 30 percent of our genes with a banana. So can the banana help us understand ourselves?"[31]

—**Denyse O'Leary,** science journalist

Richard Dawkins agrees: "In the universe of blind physical forces and genetic replication, some people are going to get hurt, and other people are going to get lucky; and you won't find any rhyme or reason to it, nor any justice. The universe we observe has precisely the properties we should expect if there is at the bottom, no design, no purpose, no evil and no good. Nothing but blind pitiless indifference. DNA neither knows nor cares. DNA just is, and we dance to its music."[32]

THE FOSSIL RECORD

SCIENTISTS SAY THAT THE PROOF for evolution can be found in the fossil record. Because evolution is said to take place gradually over a very long period of time, the only place where we might expect to see the evidence of evolution would be in the geologic column, which would preserve the many organisms that have lived on this planet.

The fossil record certainly proves that a wide variety of organisms populated the earth in the past. Most of these organisms no longer exist and are known only by their fossils. But does the fossil record prove evolution? That is a question I addressed 30 years ago in my book *Fossils in Focus*.[1] The fossil evidence then, and the fossil evidence now, is certainly not very persuasive.

To understand this we need to go back to the nineteenth century, when Charles Darwin wrote *On the Origin of Species*. Paleontologists had been collecting fossils and trying to make sense of them. And after the publication of his treatise, they became even more diligent in the collecting and cataloging of their finds. When I was at Yale University, I had an office in what used to be the home of Othneil Charles Marsh. In 1866, Marsh was appointed to Yale's chair of paleontology (the first such appointment made in this country). He and other paleontologists worked hard to provide evidence for Charles Darwin's theory.

There was a good reason for this. Darwin realized that the fossil record in his day did not seem to support his theory. If evolution was true, then the fossil record should have been full of intermediate forms bridging the gap between one organism and another. At the time in which he wrote, paleontologists were not able to find these intermediate links. Darwin therefore asked:

> Why then is not every geological formation and every stratum full of such intermediate links? Geology assuredly does not reveal any such finely graduated organic chain; and this, perhaps is the most obvious and serious objection which can be urged against the theory. The explanation lives, as I believe, in the extreme imperfection of the geological record.[2]

He assumed that the geologic record was imperfect, but still held out for the possibility that eventually we would find some of the "missing links."

"When discussing organic evolution the only point of agreement seems to be: 'It happened.' Thereafter, there is little consensus, which at first sight must seem rather odd."[3]

—Simon Conway Morris,
paleontologist at the University of Cambridge

Have scientists found the missing links predicted by Darwin?

After more than a century of research and work, most of the missing links Charles Darwin talked about are still missing. When I first wrote about this 30 years ago, I quoted from evolutionists to make the case that there were significant gaps in the fossil record.

Evolutionist George Gaylord Simpson, for example, acknowledged that "it is a feature of the known fossil record that most taxa appear abruptly. They are not, as a rule, led up to by a sequence of almost imperceptibly changing forerunners such as Darwin believed should be usual in evolution."[4]

Paleontologist David Kitts, writing in the journal *Evolution,* also observed this striking absence of intermediate links in the fossil record:

> Despite the bright promise that paleontology provides a means of "seeing" evolution, it has presented some nasty difficulties for evolutionists, the most notorious of which is the presence of "gaps" in the fossil record. Evolution requires intermediate forms between species and paleontology does not provide them.[5]

Even 30 years ago, we were beginning to notice an interesting phenomenon. It turned out that the more fossils that were found in the geologic column, the more pronounced the gaps appeared. Norman Newell of the American Museum of Natural History described the situation this way: "Experience shows us that the gaps which separate the highest categories may never be bridged in the fossil record. Many of the discontinuities tend to be more and more emphasized with increased collecting."[6]

What have we found in the last 30 years? David Raup, writing in the bulletin of the Field Museum of Natural History, acknowledged,

> The record of evolution is still surprisingly jerky and, ironically, we have even fewer examples of evolutionary transition than we had in Darwin's time. By this I mean

that the classic cases of Darwinian change in the fossil record, such as the evolution of the horse in North America, have had to be modified or discarded as a result of more detailed information.[7]

That is an incredible admission. Today, there are fewer examples of evolutionary transition than existed during Darwin's day. That is not what evolutionists and paleontologists expected.

"Can you tell me anything you know about evolution, any one thing that is true? I tried this question on the geology staff at the Field Museum of Natural History and the only answer I got was silence. I tried it on the members of the Evolutionary Morphology seminar in the University of Chicago, a very prestigious body of evolution-ists, and all I got there was silence for a long time but eventually one person said, 'I do know one thing—it ought not to be taught in high school.' Then I woke up and realized that all my life I had been duped into taking evolutionism as revealed truth in some way."[8]

—**Dr. Colin Patterson,** paleontologist at the British Museum of Natural History

---

Niles Eldredge expressed this frustration on the part of pale-ontologists who were looking for evidence of evolution in the fossil record:

No wonder paleontologists shied away from evolution for so long. It never seemed to happen…When we do see the introduction of evolutionary novelty, it usually shows up with a bang, and often with no firm evidence that the fossils did not evolve elsewhere! Evolution cannot forever be going on somewhere else. Yet that's how the fossil record has struck many a forlorn paleontologist looking to learn something about evolution.[9]

Harvard paleontologist Stephen Jay Gould referred to the "extreme rarity of transitional fossils" as the "trade secret of paleontology."[10] That is one reason he and Niles Eldredge proposed a different theory of evolution (known as punctuated equilibrium) in an effort to explain the fossil record. We will discuss this theory later in this chapter.

What about the Cambrian explosion of life?

Charles Darwin also acknowledged in *On the Origin of Species* that another challenge to his theory was the Cambrian explosion of life. At the time in which he wrote, the oldest known fossils were discovered in rock sediments known as the Cambrian (named after rocks found in Cambria, Wales). The problem with the theory he was proposing back in the nineteenth century was that a vast number of creatures appeared suddenly in the Cambrian strata. Darwin realized that if his theory was true, there should have been many ancestors to the living forms found in the Cambrian period "and that during these vast, yet quite unknown periods of time, the world swarmed with living creatures."[11]

Darwin acknowledged that the absence of these primitive organisms in the fossil record created a problem for his theory. He said, "The manner in which species belonging to several of the main divisions of the animal kingdom suddenly appear in the lowest known fossiliferous rocks...may be truly urged as a valid argument against the views here entertained."[12] He discounted the problem by suggesting that the ancestors to these organisms may have been too small or too delicate to be preserved. Elsewhere, he also suggested that more digging would eventually uncover these missing transitional fossils.

Modern paleontologists now recognize that the sudden appearance of half of the major animal phyla in the Cambrian period is "the single most spectacular phenomenon evident in the fossil record."[13] It has earned titles such as "The Big Bang of Animal Evolution" (in *Scientific American*) and "Evolution's Big Bang" (in *Science*).[14]

If anything, the problem is worse than in the days of Charles Darwin. This explosion of life takes place in a relatively short period of time (geologically speaking). Chinese paleontologist Jun-Yuan Chen explains that when compared to the geological history of the earth, this Cambrian explosion "can be likened to one minute in 24 hours of one day."[15]

If evolution is supposed to have taken place gradually over long periods of time, the Cambrian explosion seems to be a direct contradiction. Geologist Samuel Bowring helped pinpoint this very short time frame of the Cambrian explosion. But he also noted the significant discomfort the Cambrian explosion gives to his fellow evolutionists. "We now know how fast fast is," grins Bowring. "And what I like to ask my biologist friends is, How fast can evolution get before they start feeling uncomfortable?"[16]

The breadth of diversity is also significant. Half of the known animal phyla make their first appearance during the Cambrian explosion. And some scientists believe that many other phyla also came into existence during this time. One team of evolutionists now speculate, "All living phyla may have originated by the end of the [Cambrian] explosion."[17]

Charles Darwin assumed that fossils before the Cambrian era were too small to be preserved, but now paleontologists have discovered microfossils of bacteria in those rocks.[18] So it is unlikely that the fossils could have been too delicate to be preserved. The fossils in the Cambrian strata have preserved the soft parts of animals, and there is no reason to believe that delicate organisms and their parts would not also be preserved. Cambridge University paleontologist Simon Conway Morris states this about Cambrian fossils: "The remarkable fossils reveal not only their outlines but sometimes even internal organs such as the intestines or muscles."[19]

UCLA professor William Schopf concludes: "The long-held notion that Precambrian organisms must have been too small or too delicate to have been preserved in geological materials...[is] now recognized as incorrect."[20] The Cambrian explosion is real and not due to fossils not being preserved in the geologic column.

Do gaps in the fossil record disprove the theory of evolution? Proponents of evolution say no. A number of years ago, British biologist J.B.S. Haldane was challenged to name a single discovery that would falsify the theory of evolution. "I will give up my belief in evolution if someone finds a fossil rabbit in the Precambrian," Haldane growled.[21]

Once again it turns out that the more fossils we find, the more apparent it becomes that the Cambrian explosion was abrupt. James Valentine and his colleagues believe that the Cambrian explosion "is real; it is too big to be masked by flaws in the fossil record." They go on to say that as more fossils are discovered, it becomes clear that the Cambrian explosion was "even more abrupt and extensive than previously envisioned."[22]

How have evolutionists tried to explain gaps in the fossil record?

The fossil record shows two things: First, there is a sudden appearance of most species. The geological record rarely shows a finely graduated chain of transitional forms such as Charles Darwin predicted. Instead, they appear all at once and are fully formed. This is not what the neo-Darwinian model of evolution would have predicted.

Second, the fossil record also shows what scientists call *stasis*. Once a species appears, little morphological change takes place. Specific species appear and later disappear in the fossil record looking pretty much the same throughout time. If the organism doesn't go extinct, then it looks today very much like it looked in the fossil record. These are often referred to as living fossils.

In the past, evolutionists suggested that perhaps the fossil record was incomplete. But paleontologists have concluded that "the gaps we see reflect real events in life's history—not the artifact of a poor fossil record."[23] Another biologist put it this way:

> Paleontologists have been long aware of a seeming contradiction between Darwin's postulate of gradualism…and actual findings of paleontology. Following phyletic lines through time seemed to reveal only minimal gradual changes but no clear evidence for any chance of a species into different genus or for the gradual origin of an evolutionary novelty. Anything truly novel always seemed to appear quite abruptly in the fossil record.[24]

This is why Stephen Jay Gould and Niles Eldredge proposed a different theory of evolution in the early 1970s that more closely fits the two major observations about the fossil record. The first observation was that new species originate in a geological "moment in time." The second was that they do not substantially change during their geological lifetime.

Their theory, known as punctuated equilibrium, proposed that biological change occurred in isolated populations.[25] During these periods of rapid evolutionary changes in small isolated populations, virtually no organisms would show up in the fossil record because their numbers were small and geographically isolated. Unlike the previous view of neo-Darwinian evolution, punctuated equilibrium predicts that biological change takes place in larger, more discrete jumps, and these would effectively be hidden from the fossil record. Only after these major evolutionary changes took place would these new species expand across a geographic range and show up suddenly in the fossil record.

Stephen Jay Gould proposed this theory because "the absence of fossil evidence for intermediate stages between major transitions in organic design, indeed our inability, even in our imagination, to construct functional intermediates in many cases, has been a persistent and nagging problem for gradualistic accounts of evolution."[26]

Niles Eldredge acknowledged that the gaps in the fossil record are considerable. He notes that "there are all sorts of gaps: absence of gradationally intermediate 'transitional' forms between species, but also between larger groups—between, say, families of carnivores, or the orders of mammals. In fact, the higher up the Linnaean hierarchy you look, the fewer transitional forms there seem to be."[27]

There are a number of criticisms against the punctuated equilibrium theory. First, it is merely a patch on the existing theory and does not address the mechanism of evolutionary change. As we will discuss in later chapters, there are many questions surrounding the proposed biological mechanisms for change.

A second criticism is that the punctuated equilibrium theory is largely untestable because the major evolutionary changes supposedly took place in a time and place that are inaccessible to scientific observation.

How do critics of evolution respond?

The Cambrian explosion of life certainly fits within a model of intelligent design. In their book *Origins of Life,* Fazale Rana and Hugh Ross state:

> The sudden and simultaneous appearance of more than 70 complex animal phyla [during the Cambrian explosion] defies naturalistic explanation, especially considering that only thirty of those phyla exist today and none of the thirty are new. With more than forty such phyla disappearing and zero new ones appearing over the past half billion years, evolution's going the wrong way.[28]

Stephen Meyer argues that the rapid appearance of the primary morphological types in the fossil record is consistent with intelligent design. He believes that the Cambrian explosion is the best "explanation for the origin of the complex specified information required to build the Cambrian animals and the novel forms they represent."[29]

He also goes on to point out that there are fundamental problems with the model of punctuated equilibrium concerning its mechanism for evolutionary change:

> Despite its virtues as a descriptive model of the history of life, punctuated equilibrium has been widely criticized for failing to provide a mechanism sufficient to produce the novel form characteristic of higher taxonomic groups. For one thing, critics have noted that the proposed mechanism of punctuated evolutionary change simply lacked the raw material upon which to work.[30]

Proponents of intelligent design also argue that even finding intermediate forms does not necessarily prove evolution because fossils cannot demonstrate that these transitions were due to the mechanisms proposed for evolutionary change.

This problem was unintentionally illustrated by Ohio State University biologist Tim Berra in his book *Evolution and the Myth of Creation*.[31] According to Berra, what paleontologists do with the fossil record could be compared to documenting the successive improvement in Corvette automobiles. He noted that if you compared a 1953 model to a 1954 model then a 1954 model and 1955 model, you would see descent with modifications.

What Berra apparently failed to realize is that his argument about Corvettes actually proved the opposite. Corvettes are designed and do not descend from one another. In this case, a succession of similarities does not prove descent or evolutionary continuity. Intelligent design proponent Phillip E. Johnson referred to this as "Berra's Blunder."[32]

ICONS OF EVOLUTION

ANYONE WHO TAKES A BIOLOGY CLASS in high school or college uses a biology textbook that is certain to have a section on evolution. Open the textbook to that section and you are likely to see a diagram of a laboratory simulation of chemical evolution on the early Earth as well as pictures of fruit flies, Darwin's finches, and peppered moths. All of these diagrams and pictures, along with their descriptions in the textbook, are familiar evidences used to demonstrate how evolution occurred.

These evidences are what Jonathan Wells calls the *Icons of Evolution.*[1] Dr. Wells is a well-known proponent of intelligent design, but took time out from promoting intelligent design to alert scientists and the general public to the fundamental problem with these icons of evolution. Even though they are frequently used in most biology textbooks, these icons are false, fraudulent, or fail to prove evolution. Many of the concerns he raised have been known before, but these errors continue to be published in biology textbooks.

When I speak on the subject of intelligent design, I often point people to the critique by Jonathan Wells of the icons of evolution. Even those who believe in evolution should be concerned that most biology textbooks contain these significant errors. We are not talking about picky comments about trivial details. They are substantial errors that continue to show up in textbooks year after year. Let's look at some of the icons that are cited most frequently in these textbooks.

Have scientists been able to simulate evolution in the laboratory?

Jonathan Wells begins *Icons of Evolution* by looking at the Miller-Urey experiment that dates back to 1953. The experiment supposedly showed that inorganic compounds could create the first living cell. All of this was supposed to have taken place through simple chemical reactions that took place in a primordial soup upon the ancient Earth.

The early experiments suggested that it would have been relatively simple to produce some of the building blocks of life, such as amino acids, the components of proteins. However, the euphoria of the first experiment has been followed by a serious reevaluation of the possible mechanisms by which life could have arisen.

The original atmosphere that was proposed—of ammonia, hydrogen, methane, and water vapor—has been set aside. It was replaced by a proposed atmosphere of nitrogen, carbon dioxide, carbon monoxide, hydrogen sulfide, and hydrogen cyanide, which would have been spewed out by volcanoes. The experimenters added energy in the form of spark discharge. At the end of the experiment, a few amino acids were found in a trap at the bottom of the apparatus created for the experiment. Miller would catch these amino acids and drain the trap in order to prevent them from disintegrating. We might mention that some have criticized this feature of the experiment because it does not really simulate the conditions that would have been found on the early Earth, and such intervention seems to be a way that the researchers could coax the chemical reactions down a particular chemical pathway.

It is worth noting that amino acids come in two forms: left-handed and right-handed. What Miller and his colleagues found were a 50-50 mixture of left-handed and right-handed amino acids. But living organisms only use left-handed amino acids. So even this resulting mixture of amino acids is not what we would find in living systems.

The experiment is more than 50 years old, and yet it is still mentioned in most textbooks even though the assumptions of the experiment have been disproved. Scientists recognize that the early Earth would have had much more oxygen than the experiment assumed. Originally scientists believed that there wouldn't be oxygen on the early Earth because there was no photosynthesis taking place. They assumed that until life began, there would be no plants producing oxygen.

But scientists ran the numbers and concluded that there would, in fact, be oxygen in the atmosphere due to sunlight splitting water molecules into hydrogen and oxygen (known as *photodissociation*). Scientists have also argued that these prebiotic simulations were flawed because they assumed that there was little, if any, oxygen in the atmosphere. They pointed out that the chemical reactions that were assumed to occur would be *inhibited* by the presence of oxygen.

The few prebiotic simulations that have been successful have worked only because scientists used purified reactants, isolated energy sources, and exaggerated energy levels.[2] For example, one simulation used ultraviolet light as the energy source in the reactions. But in order for the simulation to work, the researchers had to limit themselves to using the shorter wavelengths of ultraviolet light, because the longer wavelengths would have destroyed the amino acids. Yet a primordial soup on the ancient Earth would have endured ultraviolet radiation of all wavelengths. The simulation was not a true simulation at all because the researchers rigged the results.

This is typical of the prebiotic simulations that have been done. Some may have produced limited successes but they do not realistically simulate what the conditions upon early Earth would have been like. Klaus Dose summarized the problem in this way:

> More than 30 years of experimentation on the origin of life in the fields of chemical and molecular evolution have led to a better perception of the immensity of the problem of the origin of life on earth rather than to its solution. At present all discussions on principal theories and experiments in the field either end in stalemate or in a confession of ignorance.[3]

When you look at today's biology textbooks, you will find that they often show a picture of the Miller-Urey experiment. The picture will often have a caption describing the experiment. But if you read the text carefully, you will note that the authors usually begrudgingly admit that the atmosphere proposed in the experiment is probably incorrect. Some textbooks actually misrepresent the truth.[4]

"Many investigators feel uneasy about stating in public that the origin of life is a mystery, even though behind closed doors they freely admit that they are baffled. There seems to be two reasons for their unease. First, they feel it opens the door to religious fundamentalists and their god-of-the-gaps pseudoexplanations. Second, they worry that a frank admission of ignorance will undermine funding."[5]

—**Paul Davies,** physicist and author of *God and the New Physics*

The bottom line is simple. Students are presented a diagram of an experiment that supposedly shows how the chemical origin of life took place. But subsequent experiments and research have shown that the assumptions and the conclusions of the experiment are false. Nevertheless, mention of the Miller-Urey experiment continues to show up in our nation's textbooks.

What about the textbook example of embryos and evolution?

Jonathan Wells first began to do his research on the icons of evolution when he noticed that all of his textbooks dealing with evolutionary biology contained what he called "a blatant misrepresentation." The drawings of developing vertebrate embryos lined up across the various pages showed similarities that are supposed to be evidence of descent from a common ancestor. Wells said that "as an embryologist I knew the drawings were false. Not only did they distort the embryos they purported to show, but they also omitted earlier stages in which the embryos look very different from each other."[6]

During his day, Charles Darwin thought that these drawings of embryos provided powerful evidence for evolution. He even said that the similarity of vertebrate embryos is "by far the strongest single class of facts in favor of" the theory of evolution.[7]

This idea continues to be promoted to this very day. In biology class, many of us learned the phrase "ontogeny recapitulates phylogeny." This biogenetic law means that developing embryos go through similar stages that allegedly replay the stages of evolution. So this supposedly was embryological proof of evolution.

But it turns out that the pictures were and are an elaborate hoax. German scientist Ernst Haeckel drew them in an attempt to prove evolution. He selected only five of the seven classes of vertebrates (because they came closest to his theory), and he deliberately drew the embryos to appear more similar than they really are. It was a classic case of how "evidence" can sometimes be twisted to fit a theory. In this case, it was adapted to fit the theory of evolution.

What is so incredible about this hoax is that it was exposed more than a century ago. Scientists knew the drawings were incorrect, and Haeckel's colleagues accused him of fraud. An embryologist writing in the journal *Science* called Haeckel's drawings "one of the most famous fakes in biology."[8]

Stephen Gould, writing in *Natural History*, noted that "Haeckel had exaggerated the similarities by idealizations and omissions. He also, in some cases—in a procedure that can only be called fraudulent—simply copied the same figure over and over again." Gould concluded, "Tales of scientific fraud excite the imagination for good reason. Getting away with this academic equivalent of murder and then being outed a century after your misdeeds makes even better copy."[9]

Now you would think that a hoax uncovered more than 100 years ago would certainly not make it into high school and college biology textbooks. But if you assumed that, you are wrong. Many of today's textbooks continue to reprint drawings labeled as a hoax a century ago.

What about the missing links found in the fossil record?

When Charles Darwin published *On the Origin of Species* he readily acknowledged that the fossil record was a problem for his theory. There should have been some record of intermediate forms between one group of organisms and another. He believed that "the number of intermediate and transitional links must have been inconceivably great."[10] But there were no transitional fossils available in the nineteenth century to validate his theory. Darwin attributed their absence to "the imperfection of the fossil record."[11]

Shortly after the publication of *Origin,* scientists found the first examples of a missing link in the Solnhofen limestone of Germany. *Archaeopteryx* had wings and feathers like a bird, but it also has a long tail, claws, and teeth which made it look like a perfect transitional fossil between reptiles and birds. The fossils in the limestone are amazing in the details they preserved. When I was in graduate school at Yale University I had the opportunity to examine casts of the original fossils found in Germany.

When these fossils were found, they created quite a stir. Thomas Huxley helped to publicize *Archaeopteryx* as a missing link (along with another fossil known as *Compsognathus).* And in the last edition of *On the Origin of Species* that Darwin worked on, he mentioned these fossils as confirmation of his theory.

The fossil *Archaeopteryx* appears in most biology textbooks even though there is great controversy in modern times about its position in the evolutionary tree. Birdlike dinosaurs from much later geologic periods are considered the real ancestors of birds (meaning the child is older than the parent).

Jonathan Wells also tells the story of how *National Geographic* featured a fossil of a feathered dinosaur only to later discover that it was a clever hoax (a dinosaur tail had been glued to the body of a primitive bird fossil) sold on the international fossil market.[12] He also tells the story of a group of scientists who claimed to find an identical match between turkey DNA and *Triceratops* DNA. But the identical match is more likely due to the result of contamination by a turkey sandwich in the laboratory.[13] Each of these stories demonstrates that there are some who want so much for the theory of evolution to be true that they lose their objectivity.

What about the textbook example of peppered moths?

The granddaddy of all the icons of evolution is the story of the peppered moths in England. The moths appear in two forms: light gray and dark gray (melanic). We are told that during the Industrial Revolution, city factories produced pollution that darkened the trunks of trees in the surrounding countryside. This made it easier for birds to see the lighter-colored moths when they rested on dark tree trunks, and thus the birds ate them. Later, when the pollution was cleaned up, the tree trunks became lighter again, which made it easier for the birds to see and catch the darker-colored moths. This simple story became the classic "proof" of Darwin's key principle of natural selection.

Most biology textbooks illustrate this story with photographs of the two varieties of moths on light-colored and dark-colored tree trunks. But what the textbooks don't explain is that biologists have known there are serious flaws in the story.

First, peppered moths don't actually perch on tree trunks. They are torpid during the daylight hours, and rest in the upper canopies of trees. The moths in the experiment were released during daytime hours, and researchers watched birds eat the moths that happened to land on the tree trunks.

If you have ever taken biology in school, you have likely seen pictures of these moths resting on tree trunks. You may have even seen a film of birds landing on the trees and catching the moths. It turns out that in order to create the photos and the film, scientists first put the moths in a freezer to immobilize them. Some researchers even glued moths to the tree trunks.

How did this "research" become such an enduring icon of evolution? Scientists accepted it for many years uncritically because they wanted to believe it and needed a vivid and visual example to support the theory of evolution. The peppered moth story fit the bill and quickly became "an irrefutable article of faith."[14] Jonathan Wells says, "Almost every textbook that deals with evolution not only re-tells the classical peppered moth story without mentioning its flaws, but also illustrates it with staged photographs."[15]

Now there are journal articles, and even books, that document the scientific scandal surrounding the story of the peppered moths. One leading evolutionist noted that the story was a "prize horse in our stable of examples." He goes on to say that when he learned the truth, it was like learning "that it was my father and not Santa Claus who brought the presents on Christmas Eve."[16]

But what is astounding is that this example still shows up with regularity in biology textbooks, even though most scientists and textbook writers know the story is untrue. One reporter even interviewed a textbook writer who admitted that he knew the photos were faked but used them in the biology textbook anyway. "The advantage of this example," he argued, "is that it is extremely visual." He went on to add that "we want to get across the idea of selective adaptation. Later on, they can look at the work critically."[17]

What about the textbook example of Darwin's finches?

Charles Darwin received his inspiration for his theory of evolution from the Galapagos Islands off the coast of South America. On those islands are 13 species of finches, which have come to be known as Darwin's finches. It's hard to find a biology textbook that doesn't tell the story of these finches.

One study found that during a period of drought, the average beak size of these finches increases slightly. The reason cited for this is that during dry periods, most of the seeds available to birds are larger and tougher to crack than at other times. So birds with larger beaks do better under conditions of drought.

I spent an afternoon looking at specimens of Darwin's finches when I was attending graduate school at Yale University and should point out that the changes in beak thickness is minimal. Moreover, the changes seem to be cyclical. When the rains return and do away with the drought conditions, both the seeds and the average beak size of the finches return to normal.

This is not evolution. It is an interesting cyclical pattern that occurs in natural history, but it's not evolution. Nevertheless, one science writer enthusiastically proclaimed that this is evolution happening "before [our] very eyes."[18]

If this is evolution occurring, then we should be seeing *macro* changes that would allow these finches to evolve into another species. But this cyclical pattern shows just the opposite. These minor changes in beak size and thickness actually allow the finches to *remain* finches under changing environmental conditions. It does not show them evolving into other types of birds.

What has been the response from the scientific establishment? The National Academy of Sciences, in a booklet about evolution (produced for teachers), failed to mention that the average beak size of finches returned to normal after a drought. Instead, the booklet makes unwarranted speculation about what might happen if these changes were to continue indefinitely for a few hundred years. "If droughts occur about once every ten years on the islands, a new species of finch might arise in only 200 years."[19]

Is this an accurate conclusion based upon the facts of natural history? It seems to be a clear example of misleading teachers (who, in turn, will unintentionally mislead their students). The booklet teaches that the beak sizes in Darwin's finches are directional and evolutionary rather than cyclical and reversible.

A column in *The Wall Street Journal* raised questions about the accuracy and authenticity of these icons of evolution. "When our leading scientists have to resort to the sort of distortion that would land a stock promoter in jail," Phillip E. Johnson said, "you know they are in trouble."[20]

Don't we have evidence of evolution in fruit flies?

According to the theory of evolution, change takes place very slowly over numerous generations. That is why evolutionists say we don't see evolution occurring before our eyes. But scientists have attempted to speed up the process by artificially producing mutations in the laboratory. Their prime target has been the fruit fly. For decades, scientists have been subjecting these creatures to radiation and various chemical mutagens to produce the kinds of mutations they believe will demonstrate evolution.

After decades of doing this, what kinds of mutations have been produced? The results have not been very promising. Scientists have produced fruit flies with shriveled wings, and they have produced all sorts of genetic oddities. But they have not produced anything that would remotely have been advantageous in nature. None of these creatures is as fit as the normal fruit fly found in the wild.

Jonathan Wells points out, "Beneficial mutations are rare, but they do occur…But biochemical mutations cannot explain the large-scale changes in organisms that we see in the history of life. Unless a mutation affects morphology—the shape of an organism—it cannot provide raw materials for morphological evolution."[21]

There is, however, one mutation in fruit flies that has received lots of attention, even though it doesn't deserve it. This fruit fly has four wings instead of two, and it has been featured in many biology textbooks. But before we go any further, you need to know something about these wings: there are no muscles that attach to them. They just hang there and do absolutely nothing. They aren't an evolutionary advance; they are a drawback because they weigh the fly down and make it less able to function in the wild.

Biologists know this, but that does not keep some textbook writers from including a picture of the four-winged fruit fly.

Though they cannot say that this proves evolution, they just can't seem to resist showing the picture. Students who don't know the background about the experiment (the extra wings were achieved by three separate mutations that had to be artificially combined) can easily come to a conclusion not warranted by the research.

One geneticist who experimented with these fruit flies for the better half of a century was Richard Goldschmidt. After all those decades of experimentation, he finally concluded that even if one could accumulate all sorts of mutations in fruit flies, one would merely end up with an extremely odd-looking fruit fly.[22]

After decades of genetic research, scientists have also discovered something else: There appear to be natural limits to biological change. In fact, biologists Lane Lester and Ray Bohlin wrote a book by that title.[23] They provide biological evidence to show that there seems to be built-in limits to the changes that can take place within a species.

Their conclusion isn't new. For nearly a century, plant and animal breeders have been aware that there are upper limits to what they can accomplish through artificial selection.[24] There is no reason to believe the scenario would be any different with natural selection.

More recent research reaches the same conclusion. While there has been significant success with changes within fixed limitations, there hasn't been the same success in the origin of these genetic types.[25] The genetic research in fruit flies shows minor changes within them, but doesn't tell us anything about the origin of fruit flies.

Doesn't microevolution prove that macroevolution took place?

Whenever the theory of evolution is challenged, evolutionists point to the peppered moths, Darwin's finches, or fruit flies as evidence. But every one of those examples affirms only *limited* variation, not unlimited variation.

When this is brought up, scientists often resort to a linguistic trick: They describe these limited changes as microevolution. Once you accept the nomenclature, the next logical step is easy to extrapolate: microevolution leads to macroevolution. If small changes take place over time, isn't it logical to believe that as these changes accumulate, they become large changes? That is the fundamental argument for evolution.

But there is growing evidence that demonstrates that these minor variations are not the engine that drives the macro changes that are necessary for evolution to occur. Evolutionist Roger Lewin, writing in *Science,* essentially said as much when discussing the findings reported at a conference on macroevolution. "The central question of the Chicago conference was whether the mechanisms underlying microevolution can be extrapolated to explain the phenomena of macroevolution." He concluded (with a few disclaimers) that "the answer can be given as a clear No."[26]

Frequently, evolution is defined as "change over time." It is hard to find anyone (creationist, evolutionist, atheist, theist) who does not believe that biological organisms demonstrate change over time. On that, there is agreement. But there is a world of difference between change *within* existing biological types and unlimited biological evolution that leads to the creation of new types of species.

WHAT IS INTELLIGENT DESIGN?

For more than two decades I have spoken at Pine Cove Conference Center in Texas. In the early days, campers who walked to the dining hall were greeted by ivy growing on the dining hall wall that spelled out PINE COVE. Anyone who saw this knew that it was intelligently designed. They may not have known who designed it, but they instinctively knew that someone had trained the ivy to grow in such a way as to spell out the name of the camp.

Those who were familiar with the camp knew that the camp's gardener (affectionately known as Tex) had trained the ivy to spell out Pine Cove. But it didn't really matter if a camper knew who had done this artistry. It was obvious that intelligent design was behind it all. No one ever said, "Isn't it amazing that the ivy on that wall grew randomly in such as way as to form the words *Pine Cove?*" People instinctively knew that those words could not have formed by chance.

Is it possible that what we see in nature that looks designed might actually be the result of random processes? Can we determine whether something is designed and not the result of chance? What exactly are proponents of intelligent design claiming from their research? What about the evidence of bad design in nature? These are among the questions we will address in this chapter.

Is it possible that nature just *looks* designed?

Charles Darwin never discounted the fact that nature seemed to be designed. But he proposed that natural selection could account for what appeared to be design. One historian said that Darwin hoped to demonstrate "how blind and gradual adaptation could counterfeit the apparently purposeful design" that seemed to occur in nature.[1]

Modern scientists do recognize that many things in nature look like they were designed. But evolutionists say these things were not designed, even though they may give the appearance of such. Oxford University professor Richard Dawkins writes about this in his book *The Blind Watchmaker.* On the first page he says, "Biology is the study of complicated things that give the appearance of having been designed for a purpose."[2]

The title of Dawkins's book is an allusion to an illustration used by William Paley to illustrate what many refer to as the design argument. If you find a watch lying upon the sand at a beach, you naturally assume that the watch was designed and is not a result of random wave action upon the beach. The numerous, interconnected parts of the watch leave a clear clue that it was designed.

Dawkins argues that what looks like design is rather the result of a "blind watchmaker"—namely, natural selection. According to him, the various aspects of living systems are the chance result of a blind and random process that by accident produces things that can have a functional purpose. If this chance process produces something that is not useful, that something is quickly eliminated by natural selection.

Many years before, George Gaylord Simpson expressed these

same ideas. He agreed that various machines (such as a telescope, a telephone, a typewriter) are complex structures that serve a particular function. Likewise, complex organs in animals (such as an eye, an ear, a hand) also look as if they were made for a purpose. He concluded, "The appearance of purposefulness is pervading in nature." But he hastened to add that natural selection "achieves the aspect of purpose without the intervention of a purposer, and it has produced a vast plan without the concurrent action of a planner."[3]

The proponents of intelligent design argue that if things *look* designed, perhaps they are. The task of these proponents is to show how the premise of intelligent design better fits the facts than the Darwinian theory of evolution.

What is the scientific foundation of intelligent design?

Mathematician and philosopher William Dembski defines intelligent design in this way:

> As a theory of biological origins and development, intelligent design's central claim is that only intelligent causes adequately explain the complex, information-rich structures of biology and that these causes are empirically detectable. To say intelligent causes are empirically detectable is to say there exist well-defined methods that, based on observable features of the world, can reliably distinguish intelligent causes from undirected natural causes.[4]

Notice that the argument for intelligent design is not what some have called a "God-of-the-gaps" argument. When someone in the past could not understand the scientific basis for certain phenomena (planetary orbits, lightning), they placed these in the realm of God or the gods. But as science found explanations for

Point of View: It seems to me that one of the problems with the intelligent design debate is that it is often defined by its critics rather than by its proponents and so people get off track. So let me ask a proponent to define intelligent design.

Ray Bohlin: It is often frustrating that not only do the opponents define it themselves, but the media also let the opponents (or adversaries) define what it is. And often what they are saying is that proponents of intelligent design are looking at the natural world and simply—with a sense of incredulity—saying these things are too complicated to have happened by natural process or by chance. Therefore, it must be God. That's a highly simplified and inaccurate definition.

Intelligent design is two things. First, it is a challenge to natural processes and Darwinism in the origin of life and especially complex life. It is challenging whether mutation and natural selection are sufficient for what we see.

Second, it really is a scientific research program that's looking at the effects of intelligent causes. In looking at the effects of intelligent causes, do we find those same kinds of effects in the natural world?

Jay Richards: It's really not that hard to define. Design theorists essentially claim two things. We can detect the activities of intelligent agents by their effects. You are doing it right now listening to me. We do it when you read text or when we look at a road sign.

The more controversial claim of intelligent design (that can get you denied tenure at a major university) is that we can see those same effects in the natural world. So there are some things in nature that are better explained in terms of an intelligent agency than in terms of some impersonal process like Darwinian evolution. It takes twenty seconds to describe. Critics should be able to do that, but the hostility to these ideas is so intense that it is difficult to even agree on a simple definition.

Interview with **Dr. Ray Bohlin** and **Dr. Jay Richards**
on *Point of View* radio talk show[5]

these observations, the need for a god to "explain" the phenomena was reduced to smaller and smaller gaps.

The search for intelligent design is a significant part of certain scientific investigations. Archaeologists, for example, use chip marks and shape to determine whether a stone found at an archaeological dig resulted from erosion or was designed by an ancient toolmaker. Medical examiners and crime scene investigators are trained to distinguish between natural or accidental death and murder. Firefighters and arson investigators look for distinguishing characteristics at the scene of a fire to determine if the fire was accidental or arson. Intelligent design proponents suggest using similar tools to distinguish chance from design.

Consider the sculpture atop Mount Rushmore. We have direct evidence that it was designed. There are eyewitnesses who saw sculptor Gutzon Borglum spend a significant part of his life designing and fashioning the faces of the four presidents. But even if there was no direct evidence, anyone who sees the sculpture would know that it was designed and not the result of wind and erosion. The patterns evident in the sculpture constitute signs of intelligence.

William Dembski distinguishes between the mechanisms of chance and the evidence for design:

> Naturalistic evolution holds that material mechanisms alone are responsible for evolution (the chief of these being the Darwinian mechanism of random variation and natural selection). Intelligent design, by contrast, holds that material mechanisms are capable of only limited evolutionary change and that any substantial evolutionary change would require input from a designing intelligence. Moreover, intelligent design maintains that the input of intelligence into biological systems is empirically detectable, that is, it is detectable by observation

through the methods of science. For intelligent design the crucial question therefore is not whether organisms emerged through an evolutionary process or suddenly from scratch, but whether a designing intelligence made a discernible difference regardless how organisms emerged.[6]

Can we determine if something is designed?

Although we all seem to know instinctively when something is designed, that doesn't mean our instincts are the only "proof" we can use to argue in support of intelligent design. For example, William Dembski has written articles and books that provide a "filter" for determining whether things in nature are the result of regular patterns, chance, or design.

In his book *The Design Inference,* Dembski says that whenever we are confronted by an event in nature, we can attribute it to one of three possible explanations: regularity, chance, and design. He therefore concludes, "To attribute an event to design is to say that it cannot reasonably be referred to either regularity or chance."[7] The design inference consists of first ruling out regularity and then ruling out chance.

Regularity can be anything from random ocean wave actions that produce ripples in the sand on a beach to the structure of a crystal. The regular pattern is produced again and again. A regular pattern can also be generated by a computer. Suppose you wrote a program that requires that the letter *d* be followed by an *e,* then an *s,* then an *i,* then a *g,* and then an *n.* The result would be the word *design.* If there were a loop in the program, it would continue to print out the word *design* over and over again. There isn't much information that comes from repeating the word *design.*

Chance can be anything that results from random interactions. Imagine using the lettered tiles from the game *Scrabble* and dumping them on a table. It is possible that among all the tiles scattered on the table, a meaningful word might have been formed by chance. Most likely it would be a word like *he, she, the,* or *and.* It probably would not be the word *design,* and it most certainly would not be the words *intelligent design.* And you certainly would not expect to get anything like one of the sentences in this book.

At some point the level of complexity would demand that you consider something other than regularity or chance. Norman Geisler and Frank Turek illustrate this in one of their books.[8] They say that if you were to enter your kitchen and see your name and address spelled out on the table using letters from a well-known alphabet cereal, you wouldn't think it happened when your cat knocked the cereal box over. Instinctively, you would know that someone assembled those letters in a way that gave them special meaning.

William Dembski gives a mathematical definition to what we all understand instinctively. He calls this process "the explanatory filter." By asking a series of questions, a person can determine which of the three processes is responsible for the event in question. He explains:

> Regularities are always the first line of defense. If we can explain by means of a regularity, chance and design are automatically precluded. Similarly, chance is always the second line of defense. If we can't explain by means of a regularity, but we can explain by means of chance, then design is automatically precluded. There is thus an order of priority to explanation. Within this order regularity has top priority, chance second, and design last.[9]

The most difficult part of this process is eliminating chance, since improbable events do occur and may initially have the appearance of design. A chance event may be complex, but it may not have *specified* complexity. In regard to his explanatory filter, Dembski says this has to do with *specification*. He explains:

> The first objection is evident: plenty of highly improbable events happen by chance all the time. The precise sequence of heads and tails on a long sequence of coin tosses, the precise configuration of darts from throwing darts at a dart board, and the precise seating arrangement of people at a cinema are all highly improbable events that, apart from any further information, can properly be explained by appeal to chance. It is only when the precise sequence of heads and tails has been recorded in advance, when the precise configuration of the darts locates all the darts at the center of the target, and when the precise seating arrangement at the cinema corresponds to seats people have been assigned on their ticket stubs that we begin to doubt whether these events occurred by chance. In order words, it is not just the sheer improbability of an event, but also the conformity of the event to a pattern that leads us to look beyond chance to explain the event.[10]

Specified complexity is a clear indication that the event in nature is designed. Arriving at the conclusion that something was designed happens after eliminating that a particular phenomenon occurred by regularity or chance.

How does specified complexity illustrate intelligent design?

If we can identify a message as having specified complexity, how does that help us? Consider the novel *Contact* by Carl Sagan[11] (1985), which was also made into a film (1997). The story revolves around radio astronomers who discover signals from outer space that evidently comprise a long sequence of prime numbers. It doesn't take the reader or the moviegoer more than a few seconds to see the significance of the sequence. The astronomers know they have received a message from an extraterrestrial intelligence because the message has specified complexity.

First, the message is *complex*. It is a long sequence of prime numbers, and not just some random pulses from the universe. Second, the sequence is mathematically significant, and the message is independent of the physical processes that caused it. So it is also *specified*.

When the astronomers in *Contact* observe specified complexity in this sequence of numbers, they have convincing evidence of extraterrestrial intelligence. Nothing like this has been detected so far by researchers involved in SETI (Search for Extra-Terrestrial Intelligence). But if they did detect such a message, it would certainly suggest contact with an extraterrestrial intelligence.

Proponents of intelligent design argued that we can refer to specified complexity as a means to detect design. This essentially is what can be called *effect-to-cause reasoning*. Normally we reason from cause to effect, but sometimes we reverse the process and reason from effect to cause.

Normal scientific investigation is conducted in the former manner. A scientist does experiments that require observation and repeatability. He or she sets up an experiment with controls and variables and employs cause-to-effect reasoning. When investigating origins, the scientist does not have control of the causes because they occurred in the past and thus are not available to observation. Instead, scientists must start with the effect and must reconstruct its cause.

Effect-to-cause reasoning is also employed in other scientific disciplines. It can be found in archaeology, forensic science, cryptography, and even in the search for extraterrestrial intelligence. Proponents of intelligent design have applied these same methods for identifying intelligence to astronomy (see chapter 6) and biology (see chapter 7). They argue that the cosmological fine tuning of the universe illustrates design. They also argue that irreducibly complex molecular machines in biological systems also illustrate design. They believe that design in astronomy and biology is scientifically detectable.

"Natural selection lacks foresight. What natural selection lacks, intelligent selection—purposive or goal-directed design—provides. Rational agents can arrange both matter and symbols with distant goals in mind…Intelligent agents have foresight. Such agents can select functional goals *before* they exist."[12]

—**Stephen Meyer,** Senior Fellow, Discovery Institute

Is there evidence of intelligence in the genetic code?

Intelligent design proponents believe there is evidence for design in the genetic code withing living organisms. This code carries the genetic blueprints for each organism. It is responsible for organizing and maintaining the organism. It contains a high degree of information that certainly implies a level of design.

The fact that it is called a genetic *code* is instructive. We assume that when we find a code, there must have been a code creator. Even more revealing is the fact that when scientists talk about the genetic code, they use terms associated with language and intelligence. For example, DNA is *transcribed* into RNA. In turn, RNA is *translated* into proteins. Each of these words implies intelligence. And the genetic code is an informational code that requires intelligent preprogramming.

It is also revealing that when scientists cracked the genetic code, they made statements about it that implied it was the result of intelligent design. Dr. Francis Collins, director of the National

Human Genome Research Institute, announced at a White House ceremony: "We have caught the first glimpse of our instruction book, previously known only to God."[13] While we might expect Collins, who is a Christian, to make such statements, many other scientists find themselves using "code language" to talk about DNA. There are good reasons for this.

The DNA molecule is like a language with four chemical letters: adenine (A), thymine (T), cytosine (C), and guanine (G). These letters are combined in different ways to spell out a message. This message produces various biochemical substances. The discovery of this chemical code means that we can now apply various aspects of information theory to genetics. It is a digital code. Just like a computer code is made up of two "letters" (0 and 1), so the genetic code is made up of four letters (A, T, C, and G).

When we see, read, or hear a message, we rightly conclude that there must have been a message sender. We may not always understand the message, but we know it came from some kind of messenger. For example, I have lived in areas where gangs leave graffiti messages on walls and overpasses. Often I do not know what the symbols mean, but I have no doubt that they were left by someone.

Another example of messages not understood are all the Egyptian hieroglyphics found through the ages. These clearly meant something, but no one could decipher them until the Rosetta stone was unearthed in 1799. This stone bore inscriptions that enabled experts to decipher the messages in the Egyptian hieroglyphics. Everyone knew the hieroglyphics were left by various messengers, even if they didn't know what the messages said.

How do evolutionists explain the genetic code?

According to evolutionary theory, life on this planet came about through random chemical processes. Charles Darwin wrote in a letter that he believed that life arose by random chemical reactions in a "warm little pond." But decades of research trying to create life in prebiotic simulations of this supposed "warm little pond" have been unsuccessful. As we mentioned in chapter 4, scientists have been able to create a few simple chemicals (such as amino acids). But as Charles Thaxton, Walter Bradley, and Roger Olsen show in their book *The Mystery of Life's Origin,* scientists have been unable to create the larger molecules (such as proteins and nucleic acids) that are essential for life.[14] They have mixed all sorts of chemicals and used heat, electrical discharge, UV light, and so on, to no avail. We don't find organisms crawling out of the flask. In fact, we don't find much of anything that has biological significance.[15]

"We should reject, as a matter of principle, the substitution of intelligent design for the dialogue of chance and necessity; but we must concede that there are presently no detailed Darwinian accounts of the evolution of any biochemical system, only a variety of wishful speculations."[16]

—**Franklin Harold,** Emeritus Professor of biochemistry and molecular biology, Colorado State University

---

For a time, scientists thought they might have found an answer. They reasoned that perhaps these chance chemical reactions were directed by the physical and chemical laws of the universe. This idea was proposed by Dean Kenyon and Gary Steinman in their book *Biochemical Predestination.*[17] They suggested that there were natural forces that "predestined" the chemicals to line up in sequences that were biologically significant.

When I was in college (both undergraduate and graduate school) this line of research seemed promising. Perhaps there were indeed some natural laws that would be discovered that could explain the chemical reactions that lead to the genetic code and the first living cell. But as experiments were conducted to test this hypothesis, the researchers found no such laws. If anything, chance chemical reactions seemed to *scramble* information rather than *create* it. And it might be worth noting that Dean Kenyon not only abandoned his theory of biochemical predestination, but he abandoned the theory of evolution as well and became a proponent of intelligent design.

What is the probability that the genetic code formed by chance?

Now that we are learning more about the informational content of the genetic code, is it still reasonable to assume that it developed by chance? In the past, there were some simple attempts to estimate the probabilities, and the advent of computers made these attempts easier to carry out.

Perhaps the best-known attempt by mathematicians to estimate these probabilities took place in 1966 at the Wistar symposium held in Philadelphia. Mathematicians and other scientists from related fields came together to do the calculations, and concluded that Darwinian evolution was not mathematically tenable.

The chairman of the conference was Nobel Laureate Sir Peter Medawar. He observed that "the immediate cause of this conference is a pretty widespread sense of dissatisfaction about what has come to be thought as the accepted evolutionary theory in the English-speaking world, the so-called neo-Darwinian Theory."[18] When the mathematicians and scientists ran their numbers, they concluded that the probability of evolution by chance is essentially zero.

Murray Eden compared the probabilities in molecular biology

to using the alphabet to create language and noted that you can't just randomly change the letters and expect to get meaningful words. The same problem exists in biology:

> Molecular biology may well have provided us with the alphabet of this language, but it is a long step from the alphabet to understanding a language. Nevertheless a language has to have rules, and these are the strongest constraints on the set of possible messages. No currently existing formal language can tolerate random changes in the symbol sequences which express its sentences. Meaning is almost invariably destroyed. Any changes must be syntactically lawful ones. I would conjecture that what one might call "genetic grammaticality" has a deterministic explanation and does not owe its stability to selection pressure acting on random variation.[19]

The scientists also considered the need for so many favorable mutations to occur in order for any evolutionary change to take place. Once again they found that the probability of these chance occurrences was essentially zero. Stanislaw Ulam put it this way:

> It seems to require many thousands, perhaps millions, of successive mutations to produce even the easiest complexity we see in life now. It appears, naively at least, that no matter how large the probability of a single mutation is, should it be even as great as one-half, you would get this probability raised to a millionth power, which is so very close to zero that the chances of such a chain seem to be practically non-existent.[20]

Marcel Schutzenberger therefore concluded "that there is a considerable gap in the neo-Darwinian theory of evolution, and we believe this gap to be of such a nature that it cannot be bridged within the current conception of biology."[21]

What about junk DNA?

If the genetic code demonstrates design, then why do our cells have so much "junk DNA"? According to evolutionary theory, living systems are the result of millions of random mutations. So it is reasonable to assume that there would be lots of "junk DNA" in our cells, or DNA that once served a useful purpose but is now useless and thus is "junk" that continues to be carried along in the cell.

Evolutionists point out that approximately 95 percent of the human genome does not code for proteins and does not appear to be involved in cellular regulation. Certainly this would argue against design and for a random process of evolution.

Intelligent design proponents say that those who approach living systems as designed would be less likely to dismiss seemingly useless DNA as junk. Further investigation might indeed show that what seems to have no function actually performs vital functions within the cell.

For example, James Shapiro and Richard Sternberg provide a comprehensive overview of the functions of repetitive DNA—often considered to be one type of junk DNA.[22] And Roy Britten has outlined the functions of mobile genetic elements, which were also thought to be junk DNA.[23] One scientist noted that "there is still much to learn about genome structure. However, the more we learn about genomes, the more we recognize the diverse functional importance of 'junk' DNA. At the same time, we uncover more evidence for Design."[24]

What about examples of bad design in nature?

A major argument against the idea of intelligent design is that certain anatomical structures and biological functions of specific living organisms are less than optimal. Some of these structures and functions even appear to be adaptations that were originally fashioned for other purposes. Don't these examples of bad design argue against intelligent design?

In his book *The Panda's Thumb,* Harvard paleontologist Stephen Gould wrote, "If God had designed a beautiful machine to reflect his wisdom and power, surely he would not have used a collection of parts generally fashioned for other purposes." He therefore concludes, "Odd arrangements and funny solutions are the proof of evolution—paths that a sensible God would never tread but that a natural process, constrained by history, follows perforce."[25]

A similar argument can be found in a *Scientific American* article entitled "If Humans Were Built to Last."[26] The authors (Jay Olshansky, Bruce Carnes, and Robert Butler) argue that the human body is the result of a mindless process of natural selection and is not the culmination of intelligent design. They argue that many of our physical shortcomings exist because natural selection causes us to survive "just long enough to reproduce." After that, our bodies fall apart.

Proponents of intelligent design reject these arguments about bad design for a number of reasons. First, suboptimal design is still design. The first automobile and the first computer ever designed were certainly suboptimal. But no one would deny that they both were designed by intelligent beings. This argument assumes that a Designer would only design creatures that are optimal. While that might have been the case in the original creation, the Fall (Genesis 3) has changed all of that.

Second, many of the previously cited examples of allegedly bad design have been discarded. Further investigation showed that some seemingly purposeless organs (such as the appendix) have important functions. Others (such as the panda's thumb) are actually ideally suited for their intended purpose.[27] So the conclusion that cells carry so-called junk DNA now seems premature, and scientists are discovering purpose where there seemed to be none.

INTELLIGENT DESIGN IN ASTRONOMY

SINCE THE TIME OF COPERNICUS, astronomers in general have assumed that the Earth is not very special. The Copernican principle is much more than just a simple observation that the universe does not revolve around the Earth. It is a metaphysical construct that has displaced human beings from the center of the cosmos.

The late astronomer Carl Sagan made this case in his book *Pale Blue Dot.* He talked about the image of Earth taken by Voyager I in 1990 when it was four billion miles away:

> "Because of the reflection of sunlight…Earth seems to be sitting in a beam of light, as if there were some special significance to this small world…Our planet is a lonely speck in the great enveloping cosmic dark. In our obscurity, in all this vastness, there is no hint that help will come from elsewhere to save us from ourselves."[1]

Sagan is not alone is his assessment. Many astronomers assume that our location is unexceptional and unremarkable. Sagan assumed that given the vastness of the universe, it should be brimming with life. Astronomer Frank Drake proposed what later came to be known as the Drake Equation, which lists the factors necessary for the existence of extraterrestrial civilizations that could use radio signals to communicate.[2] Based on such calculations, Sagan estimated that there might be as many as one million advanced civilizations just in our galaxy.

This view, however, is changing. Astronomers, astrophysicists, and cosmologists are discovering that the conditions on Earth are quite unique when compared to what might be found elsewhere in the universe. Paleontologist Peter Ward and astronomer Donald Brownlee, in their book *Rare Earth: Why Complex Life Is Uncommon in the Universe,* discuss the many improbable astronomical and geological factors that have come together to allow complex life forms to exist on Earth.[3] But they still believe that all of this is merely an unintended fluke. In a lecture after the publication of his book, Peter Ward remarked, "We are just incredibly lucky. Somebody had to win the big lottery, and we were it."[4] Proponents of intelligent design believe there is a better explanation.

Has the universe been fine-tuned?

Astronomers have discovered that the parameters associated with the universe, our galaxy, our solar system, and Earth are intricately balanced. They are so balanced and so finely tuned that some people have said everything is essentially on a knife edge. If there were a slight change in conditions in either direction, life (especially complex life) would not exist. In many cases, the universe itself would not exist.

For example, if the strength of gravity were weaker by only one part in a trillion, trillion, trillion, the universe would expand too rapidly for galaxies and planets to form. But if gravity were stronger by one part in a trillion, trillion, trillion, the universe would collapse upon itself. Similar fine tuning can be found for the constants in equations for gravity, electromagnetism, and strong and weak nuclear forces. It can also be found in the ratio of proton-to-electron mass.

These kinds of delicate balances are among the reasons that many refer to our universe as a "just right universe." Some even call it the Goldilocks universe because the forces are not too strong and not too weak. They are just right.

Point of View: It seems the astronomers are saying that they disagree with the traditional Carl Sagan view that the universe would be full of billions and billions of planets and thus the universe should be brimming with life. Instead, they seem to be saying that it is pretty unusual that we even have this planet that is habitable for life.

Jay Richards: Carl Sagan believed something called the Copernican principle, which is the basic idea that whatever happened here on Earth must have happened countless times elsewhere. So our situation is not extraordinary. It is ordinary. So Sagan and others just expected most planets to be more or less just like the Earth, and life would proliferate.

Yet almost everything we have learned in the field of astrobiology over the last 40 years (in which we have gotten detailed knowledge of what conditions would be like in other planetary environments), we have realized that you have to get a whole lot of stuff just right. So now the debate has come to answering the question, Just how rare are the conditions for life? No one thinks you are going to get life absolutely everywhere.

Unfortunately, those on the other side of the debate, in general, are still not willing to consider the wider question of design or purpose. Brownlee and Ward wrote the book *Rare Earth* [in which] they argue for the rarity of conditions for an earthlike planet. But they just attribute it all to chance. We are just the lucky recipients of this blind cosmic lottery.

—Interview with **Dr. Jay Richards** on
Point of View radio talk show[5]

One way to imagine this is to think of the parameters of the universe as being like giant dials on a control panel. All of the dials are adjusted to favor life. One science reporter put it this way: "They are like the knobs on God's control console, and they seem almost miraculously tuned to allow life."[6]

Scientists cannot find any physical cause that would explain why these parameters are so finely tuned to support living systems. Astronomer George Greenstein acknowledges, "Nothing in all of physics explains why its fundamental principles should conform themselves so precisely to life's requirements."[7] Some astronomers wonder if there is some significance to all of these finely tuned parameters. "Why is nature so ingeniously, one might even say suspiciously, friendly to life?" asks astrophysicist Paul Davies. "It's almost as if a Grand Designer had it all figured out."[8]

Is Earth a privileged planet?

One book (and subsequent film) that attempted to bring together all of the data supporting the idea of intelligent design in astronomy is *The Privileged Planet* by astronomer Guillermo Gonzalez and philosopher Jay Richards.[9] They challenged the idea that Earth is merely an insignificant speck in a vast and meaningless universe. Instead, they set forth the case that our planet is exquisitely designed both for life and for scientific discovery. Gonzales and Richards conclude, "Mounting evidence suggests that the conditions necessary for complex life are exceedingly rare, and that the probability of them all converging at the same place and time is minute."[10]

They also argue that Earth is especially suited for scientific investigation. Because our galaxy (the Milky Way) is relatively flat, we can observe other galaxies clearly. And because our galaxy is positioned between two of the Milky Way's spiral arms, we have a relatively unobstructed view of these distant galaxies.

Point of View: You are the coauthor of *The Privileged Planet.* And it is based upon the premise of Goldilocks and the three bears—not too hot, not too cold, but just right. We find ourselves in a "just right universe," don't we?

Jay Richards: Absolutely. In the book, we talk about habitability conditions—the things you need to build a habitable planet. You need to have the right kind of star [for a sun]. You need to have the right size planet. You need to be the right distance from the star, in the so-called "Goldilocks zone," where it is not too hot, not too cold. You have to be in the right galaxy, with the right kind of elements. You need to be in the right place in the galaxy.

And then you need to be in a universe where all the physical constants that are true everywhere in the universe are "just right." You have gravity at just the right setting. And the force of electro-magnetism is set just so.

These are suggestive evidences when you are talking about design. But for Guillermo [Gonzalez] and me, what really cinched it was the realization that when we looked at all the things you need for building a habitable planet, you also end up with the best conditions for doing science. In other words, those rare little pockets in the universe where life can exist are also the best places for observing the universe around us.

—Interview with **Dr. Jay Richards** on
Point of View radio talk show[11]

Likewise, the characteristics of our solar system also aid scientific investigation. Scientists can observe a star's location at one time of the year, and then by observing its position six months later, can use triangulation to calculate the distance of that star.

How does a solar eclipse suggest intelligent design?

During a solar eclipse on Earth, the Earth's moon comes between the Earth and the sun. Essentially you could watch a *partial* solar eclipse on every planet in our solar system that has a moon. But Earth is the only planet where a *total* solar eclipse can be seen. This simple fact struck Guillermo Gonzalez as he observed a total eclipse in India in 1995.

Why is it that only the Earth can experience a total solar eclipse? The moon is 1/400th the size of the sun, and the sun is 400 times farther away from Earth than the moon, and these ratios are such that when the moon comes between the sun and the Earth, a small area of the Earth experiences a total solar eclipse, during which the sun is fully blocked out by the moon.

The scientific benefit of a total solar eclipse is significant. When the moon blocks out the sun, scientists have the ability to see and measure the sun's corona. Normally the sun is too bright for us to see the corona, but a total solar eclipse allows scientists to see and measure the light spectrum of the corona. Much of what we now know about stars comes from such measurements.

The fact that the Earth is able to experience total eclipses of the sun makes it unique among the planets in the solar system, and possibly even unique among planets in many other solar systems. This fact alone could easily be chalked up to coincidence if it were not for all the other factors catalogued in the book *The Privileged Planet,* many of which have to do with the moon.

It turns out that the Earth's moon is the right size, shape, and orbit for the possibility of human life on Earth. Without the moon, life as we know it on Earth would be impossible. The gravitational balance between the Earth, the moon, and the sun provides us with our diurnal tides that mix the waters of the oceans and helps to even out their temperatures and stir their nutrients. If we did not have the moon, the tides would lessen in intensity and reduce this mixing effect. Life would be limited to the upper few feet of ocean water because the deeper waters would have conditions unable to sustain life.

Jay Richards: It turns out that when you get things set up for a habitable planet, you also get the conditions for producing perfect solar eclipses, during which the moon perfectly overlaps the sun in the sky. The sizes and shapes of these things are a near-perfect match. This is something astronomers have known for centuries, but they've never thought about the wider underlying connection.

All astronomers know that solar eclipses have been very important in the history of scientific discovery. There are things we would have a very difficult time discovering without them. Moreover, solar eclipses, for a lot of people, are almost a spiritual experience. And some people say it causes the hairs on the back of their necks to go up when they hear that there actually might be a wider explanation. It isn't just a coincidence that these things can happen. It turns out that the best place in the solar system for viewing solar eclipses is right here on Earth. So the one place where there are observers to appreciate solar eclipses and use them for science is the one place where they occur.

—Interview with **Dr. Jay Richards** on
Point of View radio talk show[12]

How does our atmosphere suggest intelligent design?

Earth's atmosphere is composed mostly of nitrogen, oxygen, and the right amounts of water and carbon dioxide. This provides us with breathable air, which is a rare commodity in the universe. For example, the two planets closest to Earth are Venus and Mars. Both have atmospheres dominated by carbon dioxide. Venus's atmosphere is dense and impossible to see through. It also creates surface temperatures as high as 900 degrees Fahrenheit. By contrast, Mars has a thin carbon dioxide atmosphere that contributes to such cold temperatures that the carbon dioxide freezes at the poles.

Guillermo Gonzalez and Jay Richards point out in their book *The Privileged Planet* the importance of the various gases in our atmosphere. Nitrogen, for example, is necessary for life as a critical component of the building blocks of DNA and proteins. Because our atmosphere is 70 percent nitrogen, it is transparent, which allows us to have light when Earth faces the sun and dark when we face away from the sun, which allows us to see the stars at night.

Oxygen is necessary for animal life. Our atmosphere contains just enough to support life and not so much as to poison life. Oxygen is also a transparent gas, thus making it possible for our atmosphere to be transparent.

Water is obviously necessary for life. Water, along with nitrogen, oxygen, and carbon dioxide, helps to create an atmosphere that is not only breathable but is also ideal for transmitting light in the visible portion of the spectrum. The water vapor in our atmosphere also helps to create clouds over about two-thirds of the Earth at any one time. These clouds help control the planet's temperatures by reflecting some of the sun's energy back out into space.

And carbon dioxide is the major source of carbon, which is necessary for carbon-based life forms. Of course, we have just the right amount of carbon dioxide. If Earth were just five percent closer to the sun, Earth would be like Venus. We would have nothing but carbon dioxide, resulting in a runaway greenhouse effect. The planet would be uninhabitable. We can either assume that the aforementioned facts about the atmosphere are all amazing coincidences, or we can consider these are evidences of design.

What other attributes of Earth suggest intelligent design?

The Earth's size, its distance from the sun, its composition, and many other such factors all suggest design. For example, Earth's size is just right. A smaller planet would not have enough gravitational pull and would lose its atmosphere too easily. A larger planet would retain too many harmful gases (such as methane) and have a thicker atmosphere that would make breathing more difficult.

Water helps to regulate our atmosphere and provides a soluble medium for sustaining life. Anyone who has taken a chemistry class can attest to the uniqueness of water. For example, ice floats rather than sinks. All other liquid/solid pairs do just the opposite. Because of this unique characteristic, only the top layer of water freezes while life can go on beneath the surface of the ice. However, if ice sank, then all liquid water would eventually freeze, and aquatic life would cease to exist in cold climates.

In order to have liquid water on Earth, the planet needs to be the right distance from the sun. If the Earth were 5 percent closer to the sun, the atmosphere would be like that of Venus, and have dense, hot clouds of carbon dioxide. If the Earth were 20 percent farther away from the sun, it would be a frozen wasteland like Mars.

The Earth also has a magnetic field that shields the planet from the harmful solar wind. The Earth's atmosphere would be slowly stripped away without its magnetic field. It is also important to note that this magnetic shield is generated because the Earth is just the right size to maintain a hot liquid iron core. The heat from this core travels through the mantle, creating plate tectonics and electricity. This electricity generates our magnetic field.

When you consider the size of the Earth, its distance from the sun, its elemental composition, its moon, its water, and its magnetic field, you begin to suspect design. And when you add to all this the fact that the Earth is in a prime location for scientific discovery, you have to also consider design. Gonzalez and Richards argue that there's no obvious reason to assume that the very same rare properties that allow for our existence would also provide the best overall setting to make discoveries about the world around us. We don't think this is merely coincidental. It cries out for another explanation, an explanation that suggests there's more to the cosmos than we have been willing to entertain or even imagine.[13]

Therefore, they conclude that all this evidence "points to purpose and intelligent design in the cosmos."[14]

What is the probability that Earth's "special parameters" occurred by chance?

Astronomer Hugh Ross has been keeping track of the parameters that make our planet unique. His latest estimate is that there are 322 parameters that must be fine-tuned for the possibility of life on Earth. He therefore estimates that the probability of these occurring by chance in one in 10^{304}. This, of course, is an enormous number.

But astronomers point out that the universe is vast. So given enough planets, perhaps this probability is not so large. Some astronomers have estimated that there may be as many as 10^{22} stars in the universe, or ten thousand billion billion (10,000,000,000, 000,000,000,000). Now if we generously estimate that each star in the universe has at least one planet, that would give us at least the same number of planets as there are stars. To determine how many planets in the universe we would expect to be suitable for life without the help of any designer, we would simply multiply the two numbers together:

$$10^{304} \times 10^{-22} = 10^{282}$$

The number is still enormous. It means that there is less than one chance in 10^{282} (million trillion) that even *one* life-support body would occur anywhere else in the universe.[15] This is among the reasons many proponents of intelligent design argue that the evidence of the universe argues for the existence of a designer.

Recent studies also help answer another question often posed about the vastness of the universe. Those who question intelligent design ask, "If God created man and also designed the universe, why did He create billions of other stars in the universe?" We know now that the overall mass of the universe is yet another one of those key factors necessary for life on Earth to be possible. With too much or too little mass in the universe, the universe would be devoid of elements such as carbon, oxygen, and nitrogen, which are crucial for the sustenance of life. Therefore, it appears that God created billions of stars so that life could exist on Earth.[16]

How have critics responded to the evidence of design in astronomy?

Some astronomers have acknowledged that the fine tuning of the universe could argue to the existence of a designer, but they reject the idea of a creator. Astronomer Fred Hoyle acknowledged decades ago that "a common sense interpretation of the facts suggests that a superintellect has monkeyed with the physics."[17] But he concludes that this "superintellect" is probably an alien mind from another universe.

George Greenstein had another interpretation: "As we survey all the evidence, the thought insistently arises that some supernatural agency—or, rather Agency—must be involved. Is it possible that suddenly, without intending to, we have stumbled upon scientific proof of the existence of a Supreme Being? Was it God who stepped in and so providentially crafted the cosmos for our benefit?"[18]

While that statement may make it seem as though Greenstein were ready to consider the possibility of a Supreme Being, he went on to say that the "cosmos does not exist unless observed," so he reasoned that "the universe brought forth life in order to exist."[19]

Other astronomers dismiss the idea of a "just right" universe by proposing that our universe is just one of many. This multiple-worlds theory might lower the probabilities so that evolution is more probable, but there is no evidence that multiple universes exist. "The multiverse theory requires as much suspension as any religion," concludes Gregg Easterbrook. "Join the church that believes in the existence of invisible objects 50 billion galaxies wide!"[20]

David Gross, director of the Kavli Institute for Theoretical Physics, understands the evidence for the fine-tuning of the universe but is unconvinced that it means anything significant. He believes the concept is "totally emotional" and believes it is actually a dangerous idea because "it smells of religions and intelligent design."[21]

Yet a more reasonable explanation for why the universe is just right is because it was designed to be that way. Physicist Heinz Pagels noted that scientists seem reluctant to accept the clear implications of the evidence, saying that perhaps "the reason the universe seems tailor-made for our existence is that it was tailor-made."[22]

INTELLIGENT DESIGN IN BIOLOGY

IN PREVIOUS CHAPTERS we have examined how biological complexity argues against Darwinian evolution and in favor of the possibility of intelligent design. As we have already noted, this argument has been around for centuries.

But a new perspective in favor of intelligent design surfaced with the publication of the book *Darwin's Black Box* by Michael Behe.[1] He introduced a new concept to the debate and showed that the latest advances in science seemed to argue against the theory of evolution first proposed by Charles Darwin.

When Charles Darwin proposed his theory, the assumption was that the living cell was quite simple: a cell wall filled with a mass of protoplasm. Scientists back then had very low-power microscopes. So they knew little about what was inside living cells. Essentially, a cell was a black box. But advances in science and technology (such as the electron microscope) have opened up Darwin's black box and found things Darwin was unaware of.

What have scientists found within the cell?

Today we know that even a simple living cell is a maze of

complexity and storehouse of information. In many ways, a single cell is something like a small city filled with factories and more. There are factories that produce biological materials. There are transportation systems that move these materials around in the cells. There are others systems that attach these materials, and still others that recycle them. At the center of all this flurry of activity is the nucleus, where the codes, plans, and blueprints are housed and used to manufacture all of these important substances. And all of these activities are regulated with incredible precision.

It is worth noting that the intricacy of the cell has not escaped the attention of those who hold to an evolutionary perspective. Francis Crick is best known for being one of the co-discoverers of the structure of DNA. "The cell is thus a minute factory, bustling with rapid, organized chemical activity," Crick declares. "Nature invented the assembly line some billions of years before Henry Ford."[2] Another cell biologist picked up on the "cell as a factory" idea, saying, "The entire cell can be viewed as a factory that contains an elaborate network of interlocking assembly lines, each of which is composed of a set of large protein machines."[3]

So the cell is very complex. But Michael Behe went a step further and introduced the concept of what he calls *irreducible complexity*. This concept has become a powerful argument for intelligent design.

What is irreducible complexity, and how does it show intelligent design?

According to Michael Behe, irreducible complexity is "a single system composed of several well-matched, interacting parts that contribute to the basic function, wherein the removal of any one of the parts causes the system to effectively cease functioning."[4]

Simply stated, something is irreducibly complex if it is composed of two or more necessary parts that must be working together for it to function. Therefore, if you remove one part, then function is not just impaired but it is destroyed. In his book, Michael Behe uses a mousetrap as an example of something that is irreducibly complex.

A mousetrap is composed of five key parts: (1) the platform to which everything is attached; (2) a hammer, which snaps down on the mouse; (3) a spring, which provides the force; (4) a bar that holds the hammer back against the spring; and (5) the catch, which sets the holding bar and hammer.

Point of View: We might explain the meaning of the title *Darwin's Black Box*. When Charles Darwin wrote *Origin of Species* in 1859, he assumed that the cell was just a piece of protoplasm. But now that we have opened the box, we know how much more complex it is inside the cell, don't we?

Paul Nelson: An interesting thought experiment is to ask what Charles Darwin would say if we could put him in a time machine and bring him to the present and show him just a few of these molecular machines. If I had to pick one, it would be the ribosome. This is a huge molecular factory that builds proteins out of the codes in nucleic acids. Put that in front of Charles Darwin and ask, "Does this look like the sort of thing that could come together spontaneously on the early Earth?" I think the whole debate would be very different.

Ray Bohlin: I have made the point that there was so little that was understood about the cell [when Darwin wrote]. And Darwin was very fair. He offered different possibilities that...would put his theory aside. Michael Behe quotes from Darwin, who said that if you could find any biological structure could not come about through slow, successive steps, Darwin's theory would absolutely fall apart. The reality is that we have hundreds of those today.

—Interview with **Dr. Paul Nelson** and **Dr. Ray Bohlin**
on *Point of View* radio talk show[5]

If you remove any one of these parts, the mousetrap doesn't function at all. All five parts are necessary for the device to function. Behe makes the case that you can't build a mousetrap by natural selection. In other words, you can't add one piece at a time and expect it to function. The mousetrap doesn't work until it has all five parts. You can't build it piecemeal by the process that supposedly drives evolution.

Michael Behe argues that what we see in something like the mousetrap is the hallmark of design. Certainly some parts could be used for some other function, but the only way to catch a mouse with a mousetrap is to have all five parts working simultaneously.

The concept of irreducible complexity is significant because it poses a direct challenge to evolution. Charles Darwin acknowledged in *Origin of Species:* "If it could be demonstrated that any complex organ existed, which could not possibly have been formed by numerous, successive, slight modifications, my theory would absolutely break down."[6] Darwin went on to add that he could find no such case that would refute his theory.

Michael Behe claimed 137 years later to have found such a case. In fact, he claimed to find a number of cases affirming that the cell is filled with irreducibly complex molecular machines that could not have been built by the process of natural selection. The cell has to function as a complete unit and cannot be built by a gradual, step-by-step evolutionary process. If just one part is missing, that renders many of these cells as being unable to function.

How does a cilium show intelligent design?

One of the examples described by Michael Behe is a cilium. *Cilia* are hairlike organelles on the surface of some plants and animals. They move fluid over a cell's surface. Cilia act like oars that row an organism through water (as in the case of the single-celled paramecium). They also help move fluid over a stationary cell (as in the cells in your lungs). The cilia or epithelial cells that line your respiratory tract work in synchrony as they sweep mucus toward your throat.

A cilium may look not look complex at first glance, but it is, in fact, irreducibly complex. There are two actions to the cilium: the power stroke and the recovery stroke. These strokes are accomplished with the help of a bundle of fibers that contain a ring of nine double microtubles surrounding two central microtubles. And there is an outer doublet with a ring of thirteen filaments fused to an assembly of ten filaments. Then there are "linkers" (called *nexin*) that join the microtubles together, as well as an inner and outer arm (both contain the protein *dynein*).

All these proteins (as well as others not mentioned here) must work together for the cilium to function. Essentially the proteins "walk" up and down the microtubles and make the cilia function. Imagine yourself walking up two ladders next to each other. You would put your right foot on the first step of the ladder to your right, then your left foot on the first step of the ladder to your left. Then you would put your right foot on the second step on the ladder to your right, and your left foot on the second step on the ladder to your left. You would continue in this fashion all the way to the top, then reverse the process on your way back down. In the case of the cilia, this "walking" up and down makes it bend back and forth.

The cilium is not just complex; it is irreducibly complex. For the cilium to function, it must have the sliding elements, the connecting proteins, and the motor proteins for them to function at all. If one of these parts is missing, the cilium does not work.

It is also important to point out that the single components of the cilium are single molecules. That means there are no additional black boxes to suggest. Cilia are irreducibly complex at the molecular level.

Point of View: How does the concept of irreducible complexity relate to functions within the cell?

Paul Nelson: Michael Behe looked at functions ranging from blood clotting to the bacterial flagellum. The flagellum is embedded in the membrane of E. coli (the organism that is found in the human gut). And he asked how the process of natural selection is going to approach these functional targets incrementally, when it appears that the function (clotting, propulsion) requires multiple independent parts all at the same time.

The book *Darwin's Black Box* sparked intense debate in the biological community. Many scientists said, "I'll take up that challenge. I'll show you how this could have happened by Darwinian processes."

—Interview with **Dr. Paul Nelson** on *Point of View* radio talk show[7]

How does a flagellum show intelligent design?

Perhaps the best-known example used by Michael Behe is the bacterial flagellum. Some have even called it the poster child of the intelligent design movement. It has also been called the most efficient machine in the universe. The bacterial flagellum is a rotary motor with a propeller and many other parts (universal joint, stator, and rotor). In some ways it is similar to a cilium in that it has numerous proteins involved in its function, and they all must be present for it to function. If you take away just one, either the flagellum is not produced, or it doesn't function at all.

But the basic structure of a flagellum is quite different from that of a cilium. It looks somewhat like an outboard motor, but this molecular motor can rotate at speeds up to 100,000 rpm. The flagellum is a long filament consisting of a single protein called *flagellin*. Near the surface of the cell is a bulge where the filament attaches to the rotor drive by means of a "hook protein."

Unlike a cilium, the bacterial flagellum has no motor protein. If the filament is broken off, the filament just floats stiffly in the water. Therefore the motor that rotates the filament-propellor must be located somewhere else. Experiments have demonstrated that it is located at the base of the flagellum, where electron microscopy shows several ring structures occur.[8]

Michael Behe argues that the bacterial flagellum demonstrates a clear example of irreducible complexity. If any of the key components are missing, the bacterial flagellum does not work. He concludes with this statement:

In summary, as biochemists have begun to examine apparently simple structures like cilia and flagella, they have discovered staggering complexity, with dozens or even hundreds of precisely tailored parts. It is very likely that many of the parts we have not considered here are required for any cilium to function in a cell. As the number of required parts increases, the difficulty of gradually putting the system together skyrockets, and the likelihood of indirect scenarios plummets. Darwin looks more and more forlorn. New research on the roles of the auxiliary proteins cannot simplify the irreducibly complex system. The intransigence of the problem cannot be alleviated; it will only get worse. Darwinian theory has given no explanation for the cilium or flagellum. The overwhelming complexity of the swimming systems push us to think it may never give an explanation.[9]

How have critics of intelligent design responded to the examples of irreducible complexity?

Some critics have responded to the idea of irreducible complexity with philosophical objections, while others have responded with scientific critiques. The philosophical objection is easy to state: Intelligent design is not a materialistic explanation for the origin of biological information. Therefore, it is not a scientific explanation. We have already addressed this objection briefly in a previous chapter, but will consider it more fully in the next chapter. It is sufficient here to point out that finding evidence for intelligent design does not necessarily require a belief in the supernatural (although for most people it does).

Point of View: You mentioned the bacterial flagellum. It seems to me that we are talking about something like an outboard motor.

Ray Bohlin: I think that is why some have called the bacterial flagellum the poster child of intelligent design. The example is used frequently, and that is because it is easy to explain what it does.

It's like a rotary outboard motor. It has a u-joint, a propeller, a shaft, bushings, and so on. When people see it, they recognize it. So when you say that this has all the same protein parts to it [that you would find in an outboard motor], you can see the wheels turning in their head. Then when you show some of the animation, people's jaws drop open.

Paul Nelson: When you look at electron micrographs of the motor, you can see the individual protein components. The wonderful animations bring those to life. They show the audience that here is something that is in your gut that is performing a very specific function. If you knock out one of the bits, you lose the function.

—Interview with **Dr. Ray Bohlin** and **Dr. Paul Nelson**
on *Point of View* radio talk show[10]

The more relevant issue here is whether the examples put forward can be explained within an evolutionary perspective. The point-counterpoint debate over these examples has been robust, as any Internet search of these examples will show. It is beyond the scope of this introductory book to describe and analyze each of the charges and countercharges.

However, let's look briefly at how evolutionists have tried to explain the bacterial flagellum and refute the claim that its irreducible complexity requires intelligent design. Scientists have found another bacterial subsystem (which is known as TTSS, for type III secretory system) that uses ten proteins that are homologous to some of the proteins necessary for the bacterial flagellum. The argument is that if we can find some of the proteins useful for some other function, perhaps during the process of evolution they were also modified to allow for the evolution of a bacterial flagellum.

First, the TTSS proteins found in some pathogenic bacteria allow them to inject toxins through a cell membrane, but the mechanism used by these bacteria has little to do with a bacterial flagellum. Scientists note that "molecular studies of proteins in the TTSS have revealed a surprising fact—the proteins of the TTSS are directly homologous to the proteins in the basal portion of the bacterial flagellum." The critics of intelligent design argue that the TTSS system was "co-opted" by the bacterial flagellum. Biologist Kenneth Miller therefore concludes, "What this means is that the argument for intelligent design of the flagellum has failed."[11]

How do proponents of intelligent design respond to the criticism regarding irreducible complexity?

The discussion and debate over bacterial flagellum has become detailed and complex. But let's consider three responses from proponents of intelligent design.

First, Scott Minnich and Stephen Meyer point out that the flagellar motor consists of several proteins that are not found in the TTSS system. In fact, they are "unique to the motor and not found in any other living system." Therefore, they asked, "From whence, then, were these proteins co-opted?"[12]

Second, William Dembski, in an essay, counters the claim by Kenneth Miller in this way: "The whole point of bringing up the TTSS was to posit it as an evolutionary precursor to the bacterial flagellum. The best current molecular evidence, however, points to the TTSS as evolving from the flagellum and not vice versa." He therefore concludes that

> over six years after Michael Behe made the bacterial fla-
> gellum the mascot of the intelligent design movement,
> Ken Miller has nothing more than the TTSS to point
> to as a possible evolutionary precursor. Behe and the
> ID community have therefore successfully shown that
> Darwinists don't have a clue how the bacterial flagellum
> might have arisen.[13]

In other words, the criticism by Kenneth Miller actually missed the point of irreducible complexity. Just because one component of an irreducibly complex system might have some other useful function does not invalidate the argument. A useful function for ten proteins that are homologous to the bacterial flagellum does not really answer the challenge put forth by Michael Behe. An irreducibly complex system requires the simultaneous appearance of multiple cooperating component parts.

Finally, Michael Behe points out that Kenneth Miller was

> switching the focus from the function of the system to act
> as a rotary propulsion machine to the ability of a subset
> of the system to transport proteins across a membrane.
> However, taking away the parts of the flagellum certainly
> destroys the ability of the system to act as a rotary propul-
> sion machine, as I have argued. Thus, contra Miller, the
> flagellum is indeed irreducibly complex.[14]

What about the evolution of complex structures?

As we noted earlier, Charles Darwin, in *On the Origin of Species,* said: "If it could be demonstrated that any complex organ existed which could not have been formed by numerous, successive, slight modifications, my theory would absolutely break down."[15]

In Darwin's day, the one example that seemed to challenge his theory was the complexity of the human eye. After all, an eye is of no use unless all of its parts are together and working in harmony with each other. Darwin wondered how the eye could have evolved and admitted that trying to explain the evolution of the eye gave him "a cold shudder."[16]

Michael Behe has discussed ways in which evolutionists have attempted to answer the question of how the eye could evolve gradually. But it turns out that the really tough questions aren't found in the eye, but in the structures inside the eye. Evolutionists have proposed that perhaps some cells with a light-sensitive spot migrated with cupped cells that focused light more directly. In other words, we don't have to have a human eye with a camera-type structure. This may have simply evolved from something much simpler that animals are able to use, because they can get by with much less.

Michael Behe points out that even this proposed first step of eye development is irreducibly complex. It requires a chain reaction of chemical processes. Oxford biologist Richard Dawkins attempts to answer this by proposing various complex systems and reactions. Michael Behe responds by saying that Dawkins "merely adds complex systems and calls that an explanation." He says, "This can be compared to answering the question, 'How is a stereo system made?' with the words 'By plugging a set of speakers into an amplifier, and adding a CD player, radio receiver, and tape deck.' Either Darwinian theory can account for the assembly of the speakers and amplifier, or it can't."[17] The foundational question of origins is how the speakers, amplifier, CD player, radio receiver, and tape deck were made in the first place.

Point of View: Some scientists believe that maybe all the chemicals just came together in some sort of biochemical predestination. Can you help us understand the specified complexity in DNA?

Paul Nelson: There are only 20 amino acids used by cells to build proteins. Proteins do almost all the important work within the cell. In DNA and RNA there are a limited number of nucleic acids that make up the information-carrying strand that carries the information about how to build these components. These are the basic parts of the system.

Now you ask yourself, How were those fairly select groups—twenty or twenty-two amino acids and four nucleic acids—pulled out by chemistry alone early in the history of the Earth? Here's the problem: The chemical processes produce hundreds of different amino acids that occur in both left-handed and right-handed forms. Only a restricted set, however, is used by the cell. So how was that selection process brought about when all you have is just dumb chemistry? This puzzle—the selectivity in building organisms out of their components—has yet to be solved by origin of life research.

In the middle of the nineteenth century, the target to be explained looked to be pretty simple. The cell was a bag of living goo (protoplasm, Huxley called it). Since then the target has gone way out of reach. You have something that is much harder to explain than it was 150 years ago. Where does the intelligence reside in physics and chemistry to build a cell? It's not there in physics and chemistry. One needs another kind of explanation, and that is intelligent design.

Ray Bohlin: There is nothing in the physics and chemistry that causes those to be arranged in a particular way. You can look at ripples in the sand (A.E. Wilder-Smith may have been the first to use this example). You can see some sort of order there. Natural processes brought that out. It's just a matter of the physical properties of sand and water.

Suppose you walk a little further down the beach and see, written in the sand, the phrase "John loves Mary." Every person, whether he or she reads English or not, will recognize that as an intelligent message. It doesn't matter if John wrote it or Mary wrote it or someone else wrote it. And it doesn't matter if it's true or false. You recognize it as having an intelligent source.

That's an analogy of what we see in DNA and proteins. It's the same kind of language and is an informational code. Those kinds of things don't happen by natural processes.

—Interview with **Dr. Paul Nelson** and **Dr. Ray Bohlin**
on *Point of View* radio talk show[18]

Are there limits to biological change?

Charles Darwin saw how artificial selection could significantly change an organism. After he returned to England from his voyage to the Galapagos Islands, he took up pigeon breeding. He was able to observe firsthand how many changes in feathers and other parts of a pigeon could be wrought from the deliberate selection of characteristics. So he naturally assumed that if these changes could take place in the hands of breeders, even more dramatic changes could take place over millions of years through natural selection.

Proponents of intelligent design say this kind of extrapolation does not hold. Centuries of artificial selection and breeding have shown us that there are limits to biological change. Botanists, for example, have been working to increase the sugar content of the sugar beet. And they have been successful in raising the sugar content from six percent to about seventeen percent.[19] But they have also found that there is an upper limit to biological variation. One scientist noted, "Some remarkable things have been done by crossbreeding and selection inside the species barrier or within a larger circle of closely related species, such as the wheats. But wheat is still wheat, and not, for instance, grapefruit; and we can no more grow wings on pigs than hens can make cylindrical eggs."[20]

When animal and plant breeders select for existing traits, they are merely shuffling the existing genes within the organism. Once the shuffling and selecting are finished, you reach an upper limit. It is like taking a deck of cards and shuffling it so that you have a hand of cards with all hearts. You can shuffle and select at will, but you will never get more than 13 hearts.

The same is true with breeding. There are natural limits to biological change. Biologists Lane Lester and Raymond Bohlin wrote a book about these limits. The book challenges Darwin's argument that artificial selection (through breeding) provides a model for natural selection. They argue that the analogy "breaks down on two counts. First, in artificial selection, there is a preconceived goal…Second, as in the case of mutations and gene duplication, all the examples of artificial selection can be interpreted as demonstrating the opposite point to be made."[21]

Breeders have known this for some time. "A rule that all breeders recognize, is that there are fixed limits to the amount of change that can be produced."[22] Botanist and horticulturalist Luther Burbank is considered one of the greatest breeding researchers, and wrote about what he called the "Reversion to the Average." He observed:

> I know from my experience that I can develop a plum half an inch long or one 2½ inches long, with every possible length in between, but I am willing to admit that it is hopeless to try to get a plum the size of a pea, or one as big as a grapefruit…there are limits to the development possible, and these limits follow a law…In short, there is undoubtedly a pull toward the mean which keeps all living things within some more or less fixed limitations.[23]

Biological change is possible, but we now know there are limits to that change. You can shuffle and sort, but you will eventually reach a limit unless additional information is introduced to the scenario. You will never get more than 13 hearts from a card deck unless you add a second deck of cards to the deck you are using. That is why evolutionists have focused on finding what are known as beneficial mutations, because such mutations would be a way of adding more material to a specific scenario and thus overcoming the natural limits to biological change.

Do mutations provide additional material for evolution?

Mutations are supposed to be the driving force for evolution, but there are good reasons to question this assumption. First, mutations occur within a gene or chromosome and are usually deleterious. Evolutionary theory is based upon the assumption that some are beneficial and that these confer a selective advantage to organisms. These favorable mutations, over time, supposedly accumulate to the point they result in evolutionary change.

Second, mutations do not add any new information to an organism's DNA. Mutations are genetic mistakes that either destroy the information found on DNA or redundantly replicate a piece of genetic information. And when a mutation *does* add new information, it is not a beneficial addition (for example, a leg growing from the back, an ear on the abdomen).

Third, for a mutation to be transferred to the next generation, it must have occurred in the reproductive cells of an organism. A random genetic change in a body cell will not be passed on to the next generation.

Scientists have artificially produced mutations in the laboratory for decades, and yet we haven't seen much biological change. The late French evolutionist Pierre Paul Grasse wrote, "What is the use of their unceasing mutations, if they do not [produce evolutionary] change? In sum, the mutations of bacteria and viruses are merely hereditary fluctuations around a median position; a swing to the right, a swing to the left, but no final evolutionary effect."[24] As stated earlier, mutations usually produce deleterious effects. And when they are not harmful, they only produce alternate forms of what already exists. New functions don't suddenly arise by mutations.

Scientists have also found that the mutations needed to change one kind of organism into another require mutations in embryonic development. But these kinds of mutations always result in a dysfunctional organism. One biologist summarized the problem this way: "Those genes that control key early developmental processes are involved in the establishment of the basic body plan. Mutations in these genes will usually be extremely disadvantageous, and it is conceivable that they are always so."[25]

One famous textbook example used to show how mutations could drive evolution involves a developmental mutation that results in a four-winged fruit fly instead of the usual two wings. In chapter 4, we showed that this is not an evolutionary advance; the extra wings don't have muscles that enable them to work. The wings perform no useful function and actually weigh down the fruit fly. The four-winged fruit flies are able to survive only in the laboratory.

Developmental biologist Jonathan Wells makes this humorous observation: "All the evidence points to one conclusion: no matter what we do to a fruit fly embryo, there are only three possible outcomes—a normal fruit fly, a defective fruit fly, or a dead fruit fly. Not even a horsefly, much less a horse."[26]

IS INTELLIGENT DESIGN SCIENCE?

WHENEVER INTELLIGENT DESIGN IS DISCUSSED, it is inevitable that questions are asked about whether it should be given a hearing in scientific circles or taught in public schools. We will deal with scientific circles in this chapter, and public schools in the next. However, we should acknowledge that the two questions are linked. If intelligent design is not science, then it shouldn't be discussed or taught in a science class. That has been the conclusion of most scientists and educators.

Is intelligent design science? Richard Olmstead (University of Washington biology professor and curator of the Burke Museum), writing in the *Seattle Post-Intelligencer,* argued:

> Science classes should teach alternate scientific theories wherever competing theories collide. However, for a theory to be "scientific," it must provide the basis for testable hypotheses. Scientists and philosophers agree—if a theory is not amenable to testing, it doesn't belong in a science classroom. Intelligent design offers no testable hypotheses and, instead, offers only an explanation for

observations of complex structures and phenomena in biology that must be taken on faith.[1]

How do proponents of intelligent design respond to the charge that intelligent design is not science, but merely religion? Does intelligent design provide testable hypotheses? Can it be falsified? These are among the questions we will answer in this chapter.

Is intelligent design science?

Scientists often assume that a theory must be based in a naturalistic framework to be considered science. This has been described as methodological naturalism. The assumption is that science must explain everything within the cosmos on the basis of natural law and natural processes.[2]

By definition, this eliminates from consideration any source or force from outside the natural world. Effectively, this is not a description of reality, but a severe limitation on the way the scientific method can be used.

Ultimately, this methodological naturalism (the stipulation that we can look only for natural causes for everything that occurs in the cosmos) leads to metaphysical naturalism (which argues that there is no God or supernatural world). By defining science as merely the search for natural causes, constraints are placed upon what can be investigated. For example, suppose miracles could occur. Science, based upon methodological naturalism, could not even acknowledge such. This limited approach to science prevents us from even considering a cause that resulted in an effect we perceive in the natural world.

Philosopher Alvin Plantinga talks about the disadvantage of using methodological naturalism as the foundation of the scientific method:

For example, if you exclude the supernatural from science, then if the world or some phenomena within it are supernaturally caused—as most of the world's people believe—you won't be able to reach that truth scientifically. Observing methodological naturalism thus hamstrings science by precluding science from reaching what would be an enormously important truth about the world. It might be that, just as a result of this constraint, even the best science in the long run will wind up with false conclusions.[3]

Critics of intelligent design argue that it must not be science simply because it has not been accepted by the scientific community. But science is not a popularity contest, in which truth is decided by majority vote. Many times in the past, a majority of scientists have been wrong. New and controversial scientific observations are rarely accepted by a majority of scientists at the beginning, but that doesn't make them unscientific.

Philosopher of science Thomas Kuhn documented in his book *The Structure of Scientific Revolutions*[4] many examples of scientific views that were modified or reversed even though the original views were confidently defended by a majority of the scientific community. But the original views came to be replaced when all the evidence was in. It is worth noting that over 700 scientists from around the world have signed a statement saying they are skeptical of Darwinism.[5]

Critics of intelligent design argue that because intelligent design has religious implications, it should be considered unscientific. But just because an idea has religious (or philosophical) implications shouldn't necessarily disqualify it from scientific consideration. As we have already discussed, there are significant religious and philosophical implications for Darwinian evolution.

- Oxford biologist Richard Dawkins believes that Darwinian evolution provides the foundation for his atheism and claims that "Darwin made it possible to be an intellectually fulfilled atheist."[6]

- Atheist Daniel Dennett says, "In the beginning, there were no reasons; there were only causes. Nothing had a purpose, nothing has so much as a function; there was no teleology in the world at all."[7]

- Princeton bioethicist Peter Singer argues that we must "face the fact that we are evolved animals and that we bear the evidence of our inheritance, not only in our anatomy and our DNA, but in our behavior too."[8]

Each of these men draws religious or philosophical inferences from the theory of evolution. Does that disqualify evolutionary theory? Is evolution unscientific because it has religious and philosophical implications? No. Likewise, intelligent design's possible implications should not render it unscientific.

Is origin science different from empirical science?

The debate about whether intelligent design is science is part of a larger discussion concerning the difference between origin science and other forms of science. Twenty years ago, Dr. Norman Geisler and I published a book entitled *Origin Science*.[9] The foundational concept in the book was that there is a fundamental difference between operation science and origin science.

Operation science is what most of us think of when we talk about science. It deals with regularities. In other words, there are regular, recurring patterns to certain phenomena that allow us to observe them, and we can do experiments on those patterns. Observation and repeatability are two foundational tools of operation science.

Origin science, however, does not deal with regularities that can be repeatedly observed. Instead, it focuses on a singular action in the past. As we say in the book: "The great events of origin were singularities. The origin of the universe is not recurring. Nor is the origin of life, or the origin of major new forms of life."[10]

We argued that "a science which deals with origin events does not fall within the category of empirical science, which deals with observed regularities in the present. Rather, it is more like forensic science."[11] In many ways, origin science is more like the scientific investigations done by crime scene investigators. A crime is usually a singular event, and often there are no observers. And crime scene investigators work with the evidence available to them in order to reconstruct the crime.

Likewise, research into origin science must use the available evidence (the bones and the stones) to try to reconstruct a past event. We therefore concluded that

> in origin science it is necessary to find analogies in the present to these events in the past. Thus, for example, if evidence is forthcoming that life can now be synthesized from chemicals (without intelligent manipulation) under conditions similar to those reasonably assumed to have once existed on the primitive earth, then a naturalistic (secondary-cause) explanation of the origin of life is plausible. If, on the other hand, it can be shown that the kind of complex information found in a living cell is similar to that which can be regularly produced by an intelligent (primary) cause, then it can be plausibly argued that there was an intelligent cause of the first living organism.[12]

In *Origin Science* we devoted a number of chapters to the rise of modern science and showed that most of the founders of modern science (Francis Bacon, Johannes Kepler, Galileo, Issac Newton) believed in a Creator and viewed nature as contingent. Thus, they developed the scientific method of observation and experimentation to study nature.

We ultimately concluded that there is a bitter irony in all of this. The scientific method we employ today was *built* on the belief in a Creator and His creation. Now, a few centuries later, the insistence that only that which can be observed repeatedly is science has been used to *replace* beliefs about a Creator or Designer being the origin of the universe and life.

Scientists have shifted their emphasis from a primary cause (God) to secondary causes (natural laws), through which God operates in the natural world. Over time, the subsequent preoccupation with these secondary causes has caused scientists to reject the legitimacy of positing a primary cause for these origin events. "In short, natural science came to bite the supernatural hand that fed it."[13]

Nancy Pearcey: Science is essentially a pattern-seeking behavior. You are looking for patterns in cause and effect. That's what intelligent design is about. Unless you know there are intelligible patterns to be found, you won't go looking for them. Critics argue that intelligent design is a science stopper. I argue that it is a science starter.

History proves that. The scientific revolution was started by people who were convinced that because God had created the universe (an intelligible, rational God), there would be a rational pattern there to find. Many historians (not necessarily Christians) now agree that it took Christianity to start modern science. Most other religions and philosophies did not start out with the notion that the universe is the creation of a rational God.

—Interview with **Nancy Pearcey**
on *Point of View* radio talk show[14]

Is intelligent design falsifiable?

One of the features of a scientific theory is the ability to falsify the data. Critics of intelligent design argue that intelligent design is not falsifiable, and thus cannot be considered a scientific theory. But is that a true statement?

First, proponents of intelligent design have set forth evidence for intelligent design as well as criteria by which their theories could be falsified. Examples of this can be found in William Dembski's books *No Free Lunch*[15] and *Debating Design,*[16] and Michael Behe's book *Darwin's Black Box.*[17]

Second, critics of intelligent design also make arguments against the plausibility of intelligent design. In other words, they cite evidence they believe falsifies the claims of intelligent design. Kenneth Miller does this in his book *Finding Darwin's God.*[18] Ian Musgrave argues likewise in the book *Why Intelligent Design Fails.*[19]

But critics cannot have it both ways. Either intelligent design is testable and falsifiable, or it is not. But the popular press has allowed critics to say that intelligent design is not science because it is not falsifiable, yet often in the next paragraph these same scientists go about trying to falsify the theory of intelligent design.

Intelligent design and Darwinian evolution are either both testable or both untestable. The testability of one implies the testability of the other. Evolution claims that certain natural and material mechanisms can account for the complex features in organisms. Intelligent design claims that some of these features are irreducibly complex and cannot be accounted for by natural and material processes. Testing the adequacy or inadequacy of these mechanisms constitutes a joint test of both theories.

Is intelligent design religion?

Some critics say that intelligent design is nothing more than "religion masquerading as science."[20] Certainly there are potential religious implications to intelligent design, but does this mean it is nothing more than a religious exercise?

During the trial in Dover, Pennsylvania concerning intelligent design, Georgetown University professor John Haught said that while intelligent design proponents do not explicitly identify God as the creator of life, the concept is "essentially a religious proposition."[21] The key point in his statement is that intelligent design proponents do not "identify God as the creator of life." One of the biggest criticisms of intelligent design proponents from certain creationists is that the former do not identify the creator. Groups such as Answers in Genesis[22] and Reasons to Believe[23] have been critical of the fact that intelligent design proponents do not identify God as creator.

As we have already shown, Darwinian evolution also has religious and philosophical implications. But that does not prevent us from looking at the facts and evidence that we're able to discern. Neither should it prevent scientists from discerning whether the natural world possesses evidence for design.

Critics of intelligent design say that a belief in such aligns with a faith position and thus makes it a religion and not a science. But the question of faith cuts both ways. Writer and medical doctor Michael Crichton gave a lecture a number of years ago arguing that the Search for Extraterrestrial Intelligence (SETI) amounts to religion because it is based on blind faith. He said,

> SETI is not science. SETI is unquestionably a religion. Faith is defined as the firm belief in something for which there is no proof. The belief that the Koran is the word of God is a matter of faith. The belief that God created the universe in seven days is a matter of faith. The belief that there are other life forms in the universe is a matter of faith. There is not a single shred of evidence for any other life forms, and in forty years of searching, none

has been discovered. There is absolutely no evidentiary reason to maintain this belief. SETI is a religion.[24]

The title of Crichton's lecture was "Aliens Cause Global Warming." I suspect that Crichton was having some fun with his audience as he criticized both proponents of SETI as well as those in the audience who were concerned about global warming. But his critique is relevant. No extraterrestrial has been discovered, so SETI proceeds on faith rather than on established fact. But most scientists would still consider SETI's search efforts a legitimate scientific endeavor. Because there is currently more evidence for intelligent design than there is for extraterrestrials, shouldn't the research pertaining to intelligent design also be considered a legitimate scientific endeavor?

SHOULD INTELLIGENT DESIGN BE TAUGHT IN SCHOOLS?

PERHAPS THE QUICKEST WAY to start an argument these days is to ask the question posed by the title of this chapter. School board candidates, and even presidential candidates, have different opinions, as do judges and lawyers. And voters have also demonstrated in many elections that they have different opinions about the question.

It is amazing what has happened in America's legal system in regard to the question of origins in just 80 years. In 1925, the infamous Scopes Trial addressed the question of whether the theory of evolution could be taught in public school classrooms. This trial in Dayton, Tennessee featured a fascinating courtroom drama between Clarence Darrow and William Jennings Bryan. In that case, the ACLU helped lift a prohibition against teaching Darwinian evolution.

Eighty years later, the question was whether a theory *other* than Darwinian evolution could be taught in the public schools. In Dover, Pennsylvania, the local school board voted to require biology teachers read a statement about intelligent design prior to the discussion of evolution in their classes. In this case, the

ACLU convinced a judge to prohibit the teaching of any theory *but* Darwinian evolution.

How did the judge rule in the Arkansas creation trial?

Before we look at the important decision in Dover, Pennsylvania, we need to look briefly at an important creation trial that took place in Arkansas. Many at the time even referred to it as Scopes 2.

In 1981, the Arkansas legislature passed a statute requiring "balanced treatment to creation-science and evolution-science." A lawsuit against the statute was brought in a local federal court. Judge William Overton ruled against the statute and argued that there is no such thing as "creation-science."

UC Berkeley law professor Phillip E. Johnson explains the ruling and dissects some of its logical flaws in his book *Darwin on Trial*. In the chapter titled "The Rules of Science," Johnson explains how the judge and the expert witnesses (such as Michael Ruse) defined science in such a way as to eliminate anything *but* Darwinian evolution as being scientific.[1] In order to limit discussion to naturalistic causes, science is defined in purely naturalistic terms. In the Arkansas creation law decision, Judge Overton said science was defined by five essential characteristics:[2]

1. It is guided by natural law

2. It has to be explanatory by reference to natural law

3. It is testable against the empirical world

4. Its conclusions are tentative—that is, not necessarily the final word

5. It is falsifiable

He concluded that creation science does not meet these criteria because it appeals to the supernatural and is therefore not testable and falsifiable.

Critics of the judge's opinion point out a number of flaws with his definition.[3] First, scientists are hardly tentative about their basic commitments, including their commitment to evolution. Second, scientists have often studied the effects of a phenomenon (such as gravity) that they were not able to explain by natural law. Finally, critics point out that proponents of creation science (and especially intelligent design) make very specific empirical predictions that can be tested. As we have already noted, the critics cannot have it both ways, especially when it comes to the topic of intelligent design. Either it is falsifiable or it's not. Evolutionists say intelligent design is not science because it cannot be falsified. Then they write editorials, articles, and books attempting to falsify intelligent design.

Phillip E. Johnson points out that the first two elements of Judge Overton's definition of science express a commitment of science to naturalism. The last three elements of his definition show a commitment to empiricism. Both of these are philosophical commitments, and not conclusions derived from scientific study.

What did the judge rule in the Dover, Pennsylvania decision?

The decision by U.S. district judge John Jones in 2005 was arguably the most significant court ruling to date concerning intelligent design. Earlier, the Dover, Pennsylvania school board had voted to require teachers to read a statement about intelligent design prior to discussing evolution in their high school biology classes. Here are some of the relevant sentences from that statement:

> Because Darwin's Theory is a theory, it continues to be tested as new evidence is discovered. The Theory is not a fact. Gaps in the Theory exist for which there is no

evidence. A theory is defined as a well-tested explanation that unifies a broad range of observations.

Intelligent Design is an explanation of the origin of life that differs from Darwin's view. The reference book, *Of Pandas and People,* is available for students who might be interested in gaining an understanding of what Intelligent Design actually involves.[4]

Eleven parents of Dover students challenged the school board decision, arguing that it violated the First Amendment's Establishment Clause. After a six-week trial, Judge Jones issued a 139-page ruling that declared the school board's policy to be unconstitutional.

His ruling was surprisingly broad in its scope. He concluded that: (1) intelligent design is not science, but religion; (2) intelligent design relies on a supernatural explanation and thus is not testable; (3) intelligent design has not been accepted by the scientific community; and (4) intelligent design has been refuted by scientists in peer-reviewed research papers.

The Discovery Institute has published a book, *Traipsing into Evolution,* that discusses the various points made by Judge Jones and provides a rebuttal to them.[5] The title of the book is taken from one of the lines in the judge's opinion: "The Court is confident that no other tribunal in the United States is in a better position then we are to traipse into this controversial area." So much for humility and judicial restraint!

Judge Jones issued a permanent injunction that prevented teachers from even mentioning intelligent design. And the injunction also prohibited the school district from requiring teachers to denigrate or disparage the scientific theory of evolution.[6] So not only was talk about intelligent design not allowed, but even criticism of evolution was not allowed.

Many wonder whether a judge with little or no training in science should be the one to determine whether intelligent design is science. It turns out that many (if not most) of his argument came from briefs provided by those who already reject intelligent design's scientific validity. One careful analysis of the opinion revealed that over 90 percent of the Judge's opinion (5,458 words of his 6,004-word section on intelligent design as science) was taken verbatim from the ACLU's proposed "Findings of Fact and Conclusions of Law."

As we have already noted, critics merely relegate intelligent design to the level of pseudoscience and reject any of its claims to be scientific. Such comments don't help advance the discussion or address the key issues. Philosopher of science Larry Laudan writes, "If we would stand up and be counted on the side of reason, we ought to drop terms like 'pseudoscience' and 'unscientific' from our vocabulary; they are just hollow phrases which do only emotive work for us."[7]

Critics also fail to understand the potential value of a different perspective concerning science and origins. Philosopher Del Ratzch, for example, argues that there are very real possible payoffs for science in considering intelligent design.[8] As we have already seen in previous chapters, intelligent design research does not inhibit scientific inquiry. It opens the doors to additional avenues of inquiry that might prove fruitful.

How should proponents of intelligent design respond to the ruling in the Dover case?

The Discovery Institute's book *Traipsing into Evolution* responds to many of the statements Judge Jones wrote in his decision.[9] Here, we will focus on three questions: (1) Is intelligent design science, (2) is intelligent design merely creationism, and (3) is intelligent design religious?

We have already dealt with the question of whether intelligent design is science (see chapter 8). Essentially, scientists (and Judge Jones) tend to equate science with what could best be called methodological naturalism. This is the assumption that science must explain the universe and all that is found within it by looking solely at natural processes.[10] We pointed out that ultimately this methodological naturalism (the idea that we can only look for natural causes for everything that occurs in the cosmos) leads to

---

Point of View: In your book *Total Truth,* you spend a fair amount of time talking about intelligent design. I know some people wonder why you put that material in there. But you understand how important the issue of design is to a Christian worldview.

Nancy Pearcey: Every scientific theory does have implications. On the one hand, science is science and not theology or philosophy. But on the other hand, it does have implications for theology and philosophy. That's where my interest comes in. I realize that for people who want to understand a Christian worldview and promote a Christian worldview and argue for a Christian worldview in the public arena, it all rests on your starting point. Every worldview or philosophy starts with certain basic assumptions.

And that's another thing we have to say against Judge Jones. He said that intelligent design assumes a Creator therefore it doesn't belong in the classroom. He totally ignores the fact that every other scientific theory depends on some metaphysical commitment, some philosophy, some starting point. The materialist starts with the assumption that matter is the ultimate reality and everything is reducible to forces within matter. The naturalist does the same thing. Nature is the ultimate reality. Every scientific theory ultimately depends on some starting point that has to be metaphysical or philosophical.

—Interview with **Nancy Pearcey** on
Point of View radio talk show[11]

---

metaphysical naturalism (which argues that there is no God or supernatural world).

Philosopher Alvin Plantinga asked whether Judge Jones merely assumed that "the dispute can be settled just by looking up the term 'science' in the dictionary." He then said, "If so, they should think again. Dictionaries do not propose definitions of 'science' that imply methodological naturalism."[12]

Judge Jones argued that intelligent design is not science because it has been refuted by scientists and because it has not been accepted by the scientific community. Yet the fact that scientists have set forth arguments to attempt to falsify intelligent design shows that it makes scientific claims that can be observed and tested. These are fundamental aspects of a scientific theory. And while it is certainly true that intelligent design has not been accepted by the majority of the scientific community, the number of scientists who question Darwinian evolution seems to be growing.[13]

The ruling by Judge Jones also implied that intelligent design was nothing more than reinvented creationism (or as one wag called it, creation science in drag). His primary argument was that the supplemental text *Of Pandas and People,* which talks about intelligent causes, used the word *creationism* in earlier drafts. The publisher said that in the mid-1980s the term *intelligent design* was not yet in use, and in a sense, the word *creation* was a place-holder term. Also, when the Supreme Court ruled that *creationism* meant literal six-day creation, the authors knew they needed to use another term.[14]

It would be more accurate to say that creationism and intelligent design are two separate camps with some overlap. Creationism is an attempt to take a literal interpretation of the first chapters of Genesis and apply it to science. Leaders in this movement include Henry Morris, Duane Gish, and Ken Ham, who are with organizations such as the Institute for Creation Research and Answers in Genesis.

Intelligent design is much less specific about biblical statements and has been embraced by people of widely divergent religious perspectives. Proponents of intelligent design place no theological requirements upon the study of cosmological fine-tuning or biological complexity. Leaders in this movement include Phillip E. Johnson, William Dembski, Michael Behe, and Stephen Meyer.

Someone can hold to a belief in intelligent design without accepting a biblical perspective on creationism. One example would be Antony Flew, formerly one of the most prominent atheists in the world. He now rejects atheism and sees intelligent design as important in explaining the origin of life.[15] He does not, however, believe in creationism.[16]

Judge Jones also argued that intelligent design has religious implications and thus cannot be taught in the classroom. But as we have already seen, Darwinian evolution also has religious and philosophical implications. But that does not stop scientists from investigating the predictions of the theory of evolution.

What about the current attempts to "teach the controversy"?

Although the decision in Dover, Pennsylvania has effectively prevented the teaching of intelligent design in public schools, another strategy has been working for intelligent design proponents. School boards in a number of states have adopted science standards that encourage critical analysis of Darwinian evolution.

Former senator Rick Santorum (R-PA) has been a proponent of this idea. In an interview with National Public Radio he said, "As far as intelligent design is concerned, I really don't believe it has risen to the level of a scientific theory at this point that we would want to teach it alongside of evolution." The senator did try to get a "teach the controversy" addendum into the No Child Left Behind bill.[17]

Some believe that the *Dover* ruling has been instrumental in bringing creation and intelligent design proponents together. They argue that

> the ruling has worked to galvanize a previously dis-
> jointed movement. Whereas many teachers and school
> boards might previously have shunned the "teach the
> controversy" strategy in favor of the more bold step of
> introducing ID [intelligent design], those groups and
> individuals are now more willing to listen.[18]

The key resource for this strategy has been the book *Explore Evolution: The Arguments for and Against Neo-Darwinism.*[19] The 150-page book has sections on universal common descent, the creative power of natural selection, and a new challenge. Each of these sections has arguments both for and against the propositions set forth.

As might be expected, the book has not been well-received by those who have been critics of intelligent design even though the book does not explicitly lay out all of the foundational issues of intelligent design. It does, for example, provide the case for and against molecular machines. But it doesn't go into the detail that a book like *Darwin's Black Box* would in describing these machines and explaining irreducible complexity. Nevertheless, the pro-evolution Internet blog *The Panda's Thumb* dismissed it as a "creationist textbook" that seeks to hide its true enterprise of "religious apologetics."[20]

Is it risky for scientists to criticize evolution?

There is growing evidence to suggest that it is often risky even for evolutionists to criticize evolution (even if they don't believe in intelligent design). A famous example occurred in 1981. British paleontologist Colin Patterson, who is pro-evolution, gave a lecture at the American Museum of Natural History in which he openly questioned the foundational evidence for evolution. He raised a provocative question: "Can you tell me anything about evolution," he asked his audience, "any one thing that is true?" For years after that lecture, Patterson received heavy criticism from the pro-evolution community. He never again voiced his skepticism in public.

Apparently it is fine to teach intelligent design if you teach it in a religion class. Professor Paul Mirecki, chairman of the religious studies department at the University of Kansas, proposed a course entitled "Special Topics in Religion: Intelligent Design, Creationism, and other Religious Mythologies."

The professor ran into some controversy when he posted an e-mail message for the Society of Open-Minded Atheists and Agnostics. He wrote, "The fundies want it all taught in a science class, but this will be a nice slap in their big fat face by teaching it as a religious studies class under the category mythology." He closed the message by saying he was trying to tick off the religious right.[21]

In the book *Icons of Evolution,* Jonathan Wells tells the story of meeting a lecturer at a conference on genes and development in Basel, Switzerland. She told him of an experience she had at a conference in Germany. There, she had made some remarks critical of neo-Darwinian evolution. Afterward, a prominent American biologist and textbook writer pulled her aside. He told her that she would be wise *not* to criticize evolution when speaking to an American audience, because they would write her off as a creationist—even though she is not. She laughed as she told the story, more amused than intimidated.[22]

Wells also tells the story of a Chinese paleontologist who came to the United States to lecture at several universities. In his lectures, he pointed to fossil evidence that contradicts the Darwinian theory of evolution. Afterward, scientists in the audience asked questions about specific fossils, but not about Darwinian evolution. When the Chinese visitor asked why, Wells told him that they were probably being polite because criticizing Darwinism is unpopular with American scientists. The Chinese scientist laughed and said, "In China we can criticize Darwin, but not the government; in America, you can criticize the government, but not Darwin."[23]

Is it risky for scientists to believe in intelligent design?

It is risky for scientists to criticize evolution, and it is even more risky to even believe in intelligent design. Some have found that doing so can kill a career. Among the best-known cases of this are Carolyn Crocker (former biology professor at George Mason University), Richard Sternberg (Smithsonian Institute), and Guillermo Gonzalez (Iowa State University).

Perhaps the best-known case is Guillermo Gonzalez, author of *The Privileged Planet.* Gonzalez has also published in prestigious journals such as *Science, Nature,* and *Scientific American.* He is the scientist who developed the concept of the Galactic Habitable Zone. Nevertheless, he was denied tenure at Iowa State University "despite a distinguished publishing record that includes 68 peer-reviewed articles."[24]

The university maintains that the fact that Gonzales has become a major figure in the intelligent design debate was not a factor in the decision. Eli Rosenberg, chair of the physics and astronomy department, said intelligent design "was not an overriding factor in the decision that was made at the department level." But John West of the Discovery Institute rejected that explanation. "His department's standards for excellence in research require 15 peer-reviewed publications. Guillermo has nearly 70." West added, "It's pretty apparent that the reason for this tenure denial is because he is a proponent of intelligent design."[25]

That this is the case is affirmed by the actions of Gonzalez's fellow scientists at Iowa State. After the screening of the film version of *The Privileged Planet* at the Smithsonian, some of Gonzalez's colleagues began campaigning against him. Since then faculty members at Iowa State (and later at the University of Iowa and the University of Northern Iowa) have signed a petition in which they "reject all attempts to represent Intelligent Design as a scientific endeavor."[26] While the petition did not mention Gonzalez by name, it was obviously aimed at him.

It is ironic that the very textbook used by the university staff in the Iowa State astronomy department is coauthored by none other than Guillermo Gonzalez. It is also worth noting that Gonzalez is being discriminated against not for *teaching* intelligent design, but for *believing* it. He says he has never introduced the topic into his classes. His work on intelligent design has always been extracurricular.

Apparently professors at professedly Christian universities are not immune either. Dr. Robert Marks is a distinguished professor of engineering at Baylor University. He launched a Web site called the Evolutionary Informatics Lab to examine whether Darwinian processes such as mutation and natural selection can generate new information. After a podcast interview with Marks appeared on a Discovery Institute Web site, the department received anonymous criticism of Marks and his research. Dean Ben Kelly (school of engineering and computer science) pulled the plug on the lab and took down the Web site.[27]

The university said that the shutdown was nothing more than an effort to comply with university policy concerning the use of

Baylor's name on Web sites. After a lengthy meeting between the various parties, professor Marks and his attorney thought everything was settled. But then the university came back and placed more demands and restrictions on Marks.[28]

William Dembski believes there is a simple explanation for why the university shut down the Web site and placed additional demands on Marks. Dembski experienced some of the same problems when he came to Baylor University in 2000 to start the Michael Polanyi Center for Complexity, Information, and Design. He saw how forces at the university derailed his plans for the center. He believes that the university president is concerned about "how Baylor might be perceived in the wider university culture if it were seen as supporting intelligent design."[29]

And all this occurred at a university that claims, on one of its own Web sites, that it is a "Christian university," and that "a necessary condition of a Christian university [is] that it bring the resources of the Christian faith to bear on the essence of what a university is—namely, its entire intellectual life and discourse."[30]

Without question, the Bible is among "the resources of the Christian faith." But one must ask whether Baylor is bringing this resource's statements about intelligent design "to bear on…its entire intellectual life and discourse."

ORIGINS AND THE BIBLE

PSALM 19 TELLS US that the heavens declare the glory of God. Romans 1 reminds us that creation reveals His divine attributes. So we shouldn't be surprised that scientists are finding evidence of design in nature. But many Christians are unsure of how intelligent design lines up with the Bible. How does intelligent design fit within a biblical perspective? Does it compromise the biblical message of creation? What are the various biblical perspectives on origins? We will consider the answers in this chapter.

Does intelligent design compromise biblical truth?

During the few opportunities I have had to speak on the subject of intelligent design, I have found that many Christians don't exactly know what to make of this research. On the one hand, they appreciate that scientists working in such diverse fields as astronomy and biology are finding evidence of design. Whether you look through a telescope at the far dimensions of space or through a microscope at the smallest details of life, God's fingerprints can be found.

Many Christians are ambivalent about the idea of intelligent design. For example, the Web sites of many creationist groups are critical of intelligent design research because it doesn't identify a creator. They want the scientists to connect the dots of their research to the God of the Bible.

If we stop there, then the concern is certainly valid. Intelligent design often presents itself as a "big tent." The recognition that a designer exists can be affirmed by many religious and philosophical groups. Saying that there is a designer does not point people to the God of the Bible. Merely establishing that there is design all around us does not tell us anything about the Designer.

But I would like to suggest another way of looking at intelligent design research. Perhaps some Christians are trying to make this research do more than it is even attempting to accomplish. Proponents of intelligent design can provide the scientific facts, but it is the responsibility of the evangelist and the apologist to connect the dots. Let me give an illustration.

Christians who defend the historical reliability of the Bible often point to the good work done by archaeologists, who have uncovered historical evidence that affirms that the biblical accounts of history are accurate. Though some of these archaeologists are not Christians, that doesn't keep Christians from using their research to show the truthfulness of the Bible. The facts of archaeology can be used to show the reliability of the Bible even if the archaeologists don't connect the dots. That work is done by Christians who weave together archaeological evidence and the biblical narrative.

We can think similarly of scientists who are doing intelligent design research. They are focused on affirming that there is design in nature. We can then take their research and show how it fits with the biblical description of creation. Although many of the scientists who do intelligent design research are Christians, some are not. That shouldn't keep us from using their research. We can take their research and connect the dots for others.

In their book *The Privileged Planet,* Guillermo Gonzalez and Jay Richards show that the earth is positioned in the best place in our galaxy for complex life to exist.[1] They also show that the earth is also positioned in the best place for scientific discovery. Christian theologians and apologists can take this research and point to the fact that God created the heavens and earth and they show His divine care.

Point of View: You have been encouraging efforts to bring together young earth creationists and old earth creationists on the subject of origins.

Nancy Pearcey: In the past, you've seen all these little groups at each others' throats. Christians have been fighting each other over these issues. The trouble with doing that is that the secular world could just ignore us. After all, if we are divided, they will surely conquer. So they haven't had to pay any attention to us.

What I really appreciate about the intelligent design movement is that it really is "the big tent." It has become more than just one more position to defend. It introduced a new paradigm that allows various groups to come together. They can ask, What has God called us to do? We are called to bring the gospel to the non-Christian world in an effective way and not to fight with each other.

To do that, we need to figure out what is the main point of issue in the non-Christian world. And the main point of issue is the philosophy of naturalism. Is nature alone capable of doing all the creating? Or is there evidence within nature itself that points to an intelligent agent beyond nature? That is the key issue.

—Interview with **Nancy Pearcey** on *Point of View* radio talk show[2]

Michael Behe, in his book *Darwin's Black Box,* shows that there are numerous molecular motors within the cell that are intricately assembled.[3] He demonstrates that they have irreducible complexity. Christian theologians and apologists can use research to show evidence of design. Design implies a designer, and the Bible tells us that God is the designer of life.

Intelligent design is structured as a scientific enterprise that has numerous religious and philosophical implications. While the conclusions do not necessarily make connections with the book of Genesis, Christians can take this evidence and connect the dots to the Bible.

It is also important to note that intelligent design does not lead people away from the Bible. In fact, the evidence for intelligent design may open the door for non-Christians to consider whether a God might exist. British atheist Antony Flew recently acknowledged that it was the evidence for intelligent design that caused him to reject his worldview of atheism and embrace the possibility that God might exist.[4] While he is not a Christian, he certainly seems more open to the possibility of the truthfulness of the Bible and may be on the road to conversion because of the evidence of design in nature.

How have Christians attempted to relate the Bible with the evidence of origin science? Whole books have been written on this subject,[5] and over the next few pages I will attempt to provide a brief overview of the strengths and weaknesses of each of the prominent positions. The three positions we will discuss are recent creation, progressive creation, and theistic evolution.

What are the strengths and weaknesses of the recent creation view?

The recent creation view maintains that the first chapters of Genesis are a literal, historical document that outlines the six days of creation and a seventh day of rest. Proponents point to the fact that the Hebrew word for day (*yom*) means a 24-hour day. Proponents also assume that the genealogies of Genesis (chapters

5 and 11) provide an accurate accounting of the history and thus suggest that creation took place a few thousand years ago.[6]

A key theological point in this view is that the creation was good (Genesis 1:4,10,12,18,21,25,31) when created. It was free of pain, suffering, and death until the fall described in Genesis 3.

"Some people mistakenly believe that one can *spiritualize* away the history of the first chapters of Genesis and that there is no harm in doing so. This will make no difference. They argue that these chapters are not history but something like parables. This type of thinking depreciates the factual content which gives information about history and the cosmos."[7]

—Christian philosopher **Francis Schaeffer**

Recent creationists say the fossil record is the result of a universal, worldwide flood (recorded in Genesis 6–9). The geologic column does not represent sedimentary layers laid down over millions of years, but instead is the result of the sorting and mixing during the flood of Noah.

Recent creationists also believe that God created various kinds of plants and animals that reproduce after their kind (Genesis 1:24-25). In other words, God created a dog from which various breeds of dogs come, yet at the same time, there would be limits to biological change.

The strength of this view is that it takes the biblical account in Genesis as true history and attempts to understand the evidence of science through a literal approach to the Bible. Proponents believe that God created the cosmos in six consecutive 24-hour days a few thousand years ago, and that the geologic column is the result of the flood of Noah.

The weaknesses of this view are as follows: First, there seems to be overwhelming evidence that the universe and the earth are much older than just a few thousand years. Second, few geologists and paleontologists believe that you can explain the entire geologic column in terms of a single universal catastrophic flood.

What are the strengths and weaknesses of the progressive creation view?

Proponents of progressive creation believe that God intervened throughout long periods of time in order to bring about His creation. Instead of accepting the creation account in Genesis as a description of six literal days, the progressive creationist accepts the standard scientific estimates that the universe is billions of years old. Proponents of progressive creation often hold to a view known as the day-age theory. This view assumes that each day in Genesis 1–2 represents a long age. They point out that the Hebrew word for day (*yom*) can sometimes mean an indefinite time period.[8] Others hold to a view known as the gap theory, in which they attempt to put all of evolutionary history in between Genesis 1:1 and Genesis 1:2.

The geologic column, according to this view of progressive creation, represents millions of years. And proponents believe that God created at various intervals and that there was probably some lateral variation among those created organisms, but not major change through macroevolution.

The strength of this view is that it accepts more of the scientific evidence than the recent creation view. Proponents don't disagree with the ages of the universe and earth. And they believe the geologic column was formed over millions of years, not during one year due to the flood of Noah's day.

The weakness of this view is theological. Proponents of progressive creation assume that there were millions of years of pain, suffering, decay, and death before the creation of human beings.

This appears to contradict the first chapters of Genesis, for death was not known upon the earth until after all of creation was completed.

Another question critics raise in response to this view is that the order of creation, as given in Genesis, does not match the fossil record. For example, flowers were created on day three, yet pollinators (such as birds, bats, and bees) were not created until millions of years later on day five.

Hundreds of churches each year celebrate Evolution Sunday, which takes place on the Sunday closest to the birth of Charles Darwin. The goal is to "come together to discuss the compatibility of religion and science." The participants believe that for too long "strident voices, in the name of Christianity, have been claiming that people must choose between religion and modern science." More than 10,000 Christian clergy have already signed The Clergy Letter, which states that the idea of choosing between religion and science is a false dichotomy.[9]

What are the strengths and weaknesses of the theistic evolution view?

Proponents of theistic evolution focus on the scientific evidence and attempt to harmonize it with the Bible. They argue that Genesis was written to show *that* God created, not *how* God created. Therefore, Genesis is providing a theological perspective, not a scientific description.[10]

Those who hold to theistic evolution point out that there is a structural framework in Genesis that begins with the statement in Genesis 1:2 that the earth was formless and void. The first three days of creation address the formless aspect of earth (God creates the light, sea and sky, and land). The next three days focus on the void (God fills the heavens, sea and sky, and land). So there are two groups of three days (first providing form, then filling the void), which culminate in a seventh day of rest. Thus, proponents argue, Genesis provides a theological pattern to describe creation and does not delineate a scientific framework.

The strength of the theistic evolution view is that it accepts the scientific data as interpreted by the theory of evolution. It assumes the earth and universe are old and accepts the geologic column as a record of millions of years of evolution. God was behind the evolutionary process (either directly or indirectly). He allowed the evolutionary process to proceed according to established conditions.

The weakness of the theistic evolution view is that it has the same theological problems as the progressive creation view. It allows for millions of years of pain, suffering, decay, and death before the creation of human beings, whereas the Bible says these things were introduced *after* the creation of humans. Also, many proponents of theistic evolution reject a literal interpretation of the biblical account of Adam and Eve's creation. Instead, they believe Adam and Eve were not real people, but are merely representative of an evolutionary process. But if they are not real, when did humans get a soul (Genesis 2:7)? And if they are not real does that mean the Fall (Genesis 3) is not real either?

Another weakness of the theistic evolution view is scientific in nature. As we have already seen, there are major questions about origins that evolution has not answered. Proponents of theistic evolution readily accept the theory of evolution even though there are many questions that still surround the theory.

How can we reconcile the various views?

I believe that as science progresses, we will find more answers to the many questions yet to be resolved in relation to origins. And I am also convinced that we will one day be able to reconcile the various views discussed in this chapter. Christian philosopher Francis Schaeffer wrote a book many years ago entitled *No Final Conflict*.[11] He maintained that when we completely understand the facts of science and have a proper interpretation of the creation account in Genesis 1–2, there will be no conflict between the two.

"I see no conflict in what the Bible tells me about God and what science tells me about nature. Like St. Augustine in A.D. 400, I do not find the wording of Genesis 1 and 2 to suggest a scientific textbook but a powerful and poetic description of God's intentions in creating the universe. The mechanism of creation is left unspecified. If God, who is all powerful and who is not limited by space and time, chose to use the mechanism of evolution to create you and me, who are we to say that wasn't an absolutely elegant plan? And if God has now given us the intelligence and the opportunity to discover his methods, that is something to celebrate."[12]

—**Francis Collins,** director,
National Human Genome Research Institute

In this book, we have set forth some of the evidence against evolution as well as some of the evidence for intelligent design. More research is necessary, and we need to remain open about where the evidence leads us, rather than hold stubbornly to theories that have been disproven.

At the same time, we should be willing to reconsider our cherished interpretations of Scripture. Francis Schaeffer said, "We must take ample time, and sometimes this will mean a long time, to consider whether the apparent clash between science and revelation means that the theory set forth by science is wrong or whether we must reconsider what we thought the Bible says."[13]

The current debate concerning origins desperately needs humility and civility on all sides. The apparent clash between science and the Bible requires us to humbly reconsider both our views about the scientific data and our interpretation of Scripture. As the research continues, let's see where the evidence leads.

BIBLIOGRAPHY

Michael Behe, *Darwin's Black Box* (New York: Free Press, 1996).

John Angus Campbell and Stephen Meyer, eds., *Darwinism, Design, and Public Education* (East Lansing, MI: Michigan State University, 2003).

William Dembski, *The Design Inference: Eliminating Chance Through Small Probabilities* (Cambridge: Cambridge University Press, 1998).

———, *The Design Revolution* (Downers Grove, IL, InterVarsity, 2004).

Norman Geisler and Kerby Anderson, *Origin Science* (Grand Rapids: Baker, 1987).

Guillermo Gonzalez and Jay Richards, *The Privileged Planet* (Washington, DC: Regnery, 2004).

Phillip E. Johnson, *Darwin on Trial* (Downers Grove, IL: InterVarsity, 1991).

———, *Defeating Darwinism by Opening Minds* (Downers Grove, IL: InterVarsity, 1997).

———, *Reason in the Balance: The Case Against Naturalism in Science, Law, and Education* (Downers Grove, IL: InterVarsity, 1995).

Lane Lester and Raymond Bohlin, *The Natural Limits to Biological Change* (Grand Rapids: Zondervan, 1984).

Nancy Pearcey, *Total Truth: Liberating Christianity from Its Cultural Captivity* (Wheaton, IL: Crossway, 2004).

Fazale Rana and Hugh Ross, *Origins of Life* (Colorado Springs: NavPress, 2004).

NOTES

Chapter 1—The Controversy

1. Matthew Cooper, "Fanning the Controversy over Intelligent Design," *Time,* August 3, 2005, http://www.time.com/time/nation/article/0,8599,1089733,00.html.

2. "Evolution Wars," *Time,* August 15, 2005.

3. Video roundtable with Sen. John McCain in C.J. Karamargin, "McCain Sounds Like Presidential Hopeful," *Arizona Daily Star,* August 24, 2005, http://www.azstarnet.com/sn/politics/90069.

4. Patricia Cohen, "A Split Emerges as Conservatives Discuss Darwin," *The New York Times,* May 5, 2007, http://www.nytimes.com/2007/05/05/us/politics/05darwin.html?ex=1190 001600&en=2e76caff6a4d8dd3&ei=5070.

5. Sam Brownback, "What I Think About Evolution," *The New York Times,* May 31, 2007, http://www.nytimes.com/2007/05/31/opinion/31brownback.html?ex=1190001600&en=186f3fd555d0a584&ei=5070.

6. Robert Lee Hotz, "The Language of Life: Sunday Book Review," *Los Angeles Times,* July 30, 2006, R3.

7. Ibid.

8. Lynn Margulis and Dorion Sagan, *Acquiring Genomes: A Theory of the Origins of Species* (New York: Basic Books, 2002), 103.

9. John Roach, "Does Intelligent Design Threaten the Definition of Science?" *National Geographic News,* April 27, 2005, http://news.nationalgeographic.com/news/2005/04/0427_050427_intelligent_design.html.

10. Paul Nurse, "US Biomedical Research under Siege," *Cell,* 124 (January 13, 2006), 9-12.

11. Speech by Kenneth Miller at Hamilton University, February 28, 2006.

12. Claudia Wallis, "The Evolution Wars," *Time,* August 7, 2005, http://www.hamilton.edu/news/more_news/display.cfm?ID=10433.

13. Richard Dawkins, *The Blind Watchmaker* (New York: Norton, 1986), 287, emphasis in original.

14. S.C. Todd, "A View from Kansas on that Evolution Debate," *Nature,* September 30, 1999, 423.

15. In this book, *Darwinism* is used to describe both the classical theory of evolution proposed by Charles Darwin as well as Neo-Darwinism, which combines the classical theory (of natural selection) with modern genetic theory (mutations in the gene pool).

Chapter 2—Darwinism and Naturalism

1. Phillip Johnson, *Darwin on Trial* (Downers Grove, IL: InterVarsity, 1991).

2. Phillip Johnson, *Reason in the Balance: The Case Against Naturalism in Science, Law, and Education* (Downers Grove, IL: InterVarsity, 1995).

3. Phillip Johnson, *Defeating Darwinism by Opening Minds* (Downers Grove, IL: InterVarsity, 1997).

4. Nancy Pearcey, *Total Truth: Liberating Christianity from Its Cultural Captivity* (Wheaton, IL: Crossway Books, 2004).

5. Pearcey, *Total Truth,* 207.

6. Edward Purcell, *The Crisis of Democracy* (Lexington, KY: University Press of Kentucky, 1973), 8.

7. Daniel Dennett, *Darwin's Dangerous Idea* (New York: Simon and Schuster, 1995), 63.

8. Nora Barlow, ed., *The Autobiography of Charles Darwin 1809–1882* (New York: W.W. Norton, 1958), 87.

9. Charles Darwin, *On the Origin of Species* (Cambridge: Harvard University Press, 1964), 398.

10. *Notes and Records of the Royal Society of London,* ed. Sir Gavin de Beer, vol. 14, no. 1, 1959, 35.

11. G.K. Chesterton, *Eugenics and Other Evils* (New York: Dodd, Mead, 1927), 98.

12. Douglas Futuyma, *Evolutionary Biology,* 3d ed. (Sunderland, MA: Sinauer, 1998), 5.

13. Carl Sagan, *Cosmos* (New York: Random House, 1980), 4.

14. Stan and Jan Berenstain, *The Berenstain Bears' Nature Guide* (New York: Random House, 1975), 6-7.

15. Mano Singham, *Physics Today,* June 2002.

16. John Rennie, "15 Answers to Creationist Nonsense," *Scientific American,* June 17, 2002.

17. Tom Bethell, "Against Sociobiology," *First Things,* January 2001, 18-24.

18. Richard Lewontin, "Billions and Billions of Demons," *The New York Review of Books,* January 9, 1997, 28.

19. Johnson, *Darwin on Trial,* 125-34.

20. Ibid., 127.

21. Steven Weinberg's comments reported in "Free People from Superstition," *Freethought Today,* April 2000.

22. "At random: A television preview," *Evolution After Darwin* (Chicago: University of Chicago Press, 1960), 41.

23. Robert Laughlin, *A Different Universe: Reinventing Physics from the Bottom Down* (New York: Basic Books, 2005), 168-69.

24. John Randall, *Parapsychology and the Nature of Life* (New York: Harper Colophon, 1977), 11.

25. J.W. Burrow, introduction in Charles Darwin, *The Origin of Species* (Baltimore, MD: Penguin, 1974), 24.

26. Michael Ruse, "Saving Darwinism from the Darwinists," *National Post,* May 3, 2000, B3.

27. Johnson, *Reason in the Balance,* 37.

28. George Gaylord Simpson, *The Meaning of Evolution,* rev. ed. (New Haven: Yale University Press, 1967), 345.

29. Stephen Jay Gould, "The Evolution of Life on Earth," *Scientific American,* 271 (1994), 91.

30. Daniel Dennett, *Consciousness Explained* (Boston: Back Bay Books, 1991).

31. Denyse O'Leary, "Deprogram," *Salvo,* Issue 1 (2007), 35.

32. Richard Dawkins, *The Selfish Gene* (New York: Oxford University Press, 1976), 133.

Chapter 3—The Fossil Record

1. J. Kerby Anderson and Harold G. Coffin, *Fossils in Focus* (Grand Rapids: Zondervan, 1977).

2. Charles Darwin, *On the Origin of Species* (Cambridge: Harvard University Press, [1859] 1964), 308.

3. Simon Conway Morris, "Evolution: Bringing Molecules into the Fold," *Cell* 100 (January 7, 2000), 1.

4. George Gaylord Simpson, *Evolution After Darwin,* vol. 1 of *The Evolution of Life* (Chicago: University of Chicago, 1960), 149.

5. David B. Kitts, "Paleontology and Evolutionary Theory," *Evolution* 28 (1974), 466.

6. Norman D. Newell, "The Nature of the Fossil Record," *Proceedings of the American Philosophical Society,* 103 (1959), 264-85.

7. David Raup, "Conflicts Between Darwin and Paleontology," *Field Museum of Natural History Bulletin,* 50 (1979), 22.

8. Dr. Colin Patterson, "Evolution and Creationism," speech given at the American Museum of Natural History in New York, November 5, 1981.

9. Niles Eldredge, *Reinventing Darwin* (New York: Wiley, 1995), 95.

10. Stephen Jay Gould, "Evolution's Erratic Pace," *Natural History* 86 (1977), 14.

11. Darwin, *On the Origin of Species,* 313.

12. Ibid., 308.

13. James Valentine, et. al., "The Biological Explosion at the Precambrian-Cambrian Boundary," *Evolutionary Biology* 25 (1991), 279-356.

14. Jeffrey Levinton, "The Big Bang of Animal Evolution," *Scientific American,* November 1992, 84-91; and Richard Kerr, "Evolution's Big Bang Gets Even More Explosive," *Science* 261 (1993), 1274-75.

15. Cui Lili, "Traditional Theory of Evolution Challenged," *Beijing Review,* March 31–April 6, 1997, 10.

16. Madeleine Nash, "When Life Exploded," *Time,* December 4, 1995, 70.

17. James Valentine, et. al., "Fossils, Molecules, and Embryos: New Perspectives on the Cambrian Explosion," *Development* 126 (1999), 851-59.

18. William Schopf and Bonnie Parker, "Early Archean Microfossils," *Science* 237 (1987), 70-73.

19. Simon Conway Morris, *The Crucible of Creation* (Oxford: Oxford University Press, 1998), 2.

20. William Schopf, "The Early Evolution of Life: Solution to Darwin's Dilemma," *Trends in Ecology and Evolution* 9 (1994), 375-77.

21. Quote from J.B.S. Haldane, http://en.wikiquote.org/wiki/J._B._S._Haldane.

22. Valentine, et al., "The Biological Explosion," 281, 318.

23. Ibid., 59.

24. Ernst Mayer, *One Long Argument: Charles Darwin and the Genesis of Modern Evolutionary Thought* (Cambridge: Harvard University Press, 1991), 138.

25. Niles Eldredge and Stephen Jay Gould, "Punctuated Equilibira: An Alternative to Phyletic Gradualism," in *Models in Paleontology*, ed. T.J.M. Schopf (San Francisco: Freeman, 1973), 82-115.

26. Stephen Jay Gould, "Is a New and General Theory of Evolution Emerging," in *Evolution Now: A Century of Darwin,* ed. J. Maynard Smith (San Francisco: W.H. Freeman and Co., 1982), 140.

27. Niles Eldredge, *The Monkey Business: A Scientist Looks at Creationism* (New York: Washington Square Press, 1982), 65-66.

28. Fazale Rana and Hugh Ross, *Origins of Life* (Colorado Springs: NavPress, 2004), 206.

29. Stephen C. Meyer, "The Origin of Biological Information and the Higher Taxonomic Categories," *Proceedings of the Biological Society of Washington,* vol. 117 (2004), 213-39.

30. Ibid.

31. Tim Berra, *Evolution and the Myth of Creation* (Stanford: Stanford University Press, 1990), 117-19.

32. Phillip Johnson, *Defeating Darwinism by Opening Minds* (Downers Grove, IL: InterVarsity Press, 1997), 63.

Chapter 4—Icons of Evolution

1. Jonathan Wells, *Icons of Evolution* (Washington, DC: Regnery, 2000).

2. Charles Thaxton, Walter Bradley, and Roger Olsen, *The Mystery of Life's Origin* (Dallas: Lewis & Stanley, 1992).

3. Klaus Dose, "The Origin of Life: More Questions Than Answers," *Interdisciplinary Science Review* 13 (1988), 348.

4. Ibid., 25.

5. Paul Davies, *The Fifth Miracle: The Search for the Origin and Meaning of Life* (New York: Simon & Schuster, 1999), 17-18.

6. Wells, *Icons,* xi.

7. Letter to Asa Gray, September 10, 1860 in *The Life and Letters of Charles Darwin,* vol. 2, ed. Francis Darwin (New York: Appleton, 1896), 131.

8. Michael Richardson, quoted in Pennisi, "Haeckel's Embryos: Fraud Rediscovered," *Science* 277 (September 5, 1997), 1435.

9. Stephen Jay Gould, "Abscheulich! Atrocious!" *Natural History,* March 2000, 42-49.

10. Charles Darwin, *On the Origin of Species,* chapter X—"On the Imperfection of the Geological Record" (New York: Random House, 1936), 234.

11. Ibid., 255.

12. Wells, *Icons,* 124-25.

13. Ibid., 130-31.

14. Peter Smith, "Darwinism in a Flutter," book review of *Of Moths and Men: Intrigue, Tragedy, and the Peppered Moth, The Guardian,* May 11, 2002.

15. Wells, *Icons,* 156.

16. Jerry Coyne, "Not Black and White," book review of *Melanism: Evolution in Action, Nature* 396 (November 5, 1998), 35.

17. Bob Ritter as quoted in "Moth-eaten Darwinism: A Disproven Textbook Case of Natural Selection Refuses to Die," *Alberta Report Newsmagazine,* April 5, 1999.

18. Jonathan Weiner, "Kansas Anti-evolution Vote Denies Students a Full Spiritual Journey," *Philadelphia Inquirer,* August 15, 1999.

19. *Teaching About Evolution and the Nature of Science,* National Academy of Sciences, chapter 2, page 19, www.nap.edu/readingroom/books/evolution98.

20. Phillip E. Johnson, "The Church of Darwin," *The Wall Street Journal,* August 16, 1999.

21. Wells, *Icons,* 178.

22. A discussion of Richard Goldschmidt can be found in Norman Macbeth, *Darwin Retried* (New York: Dell, 1971), 33, 154.

23. Lane Lester and Ray Bohlin, *The Natural Limits to Biological Change* (Grand Rapids: Zondervan, 1984).

24. The comments by Luther Burbank can be found in Norman Macbeth, *Darwin Retried* (New York: Dell, 1971), 36.

25. M.W. Ho and P.T. Saunders, "Beyond Neo-Darwinism—An Epigenetic Approach to Evolution," *Journal of Theoretical Biology* 78 (1979), 573-91.

26. Roger Lewin, "Evolutionary theory under fire," *Science,* November 21, 1980, 883-87.

Chapter 5—What Is Intelligent Design?

1. Neal Gillespie, *Charles Darwin and the Problem of Creation* (Chicago: University of Chicago Press, 1979), 83-85.

2. Richard Dawkins, *The Blind Watchmaker: Why the Evidence of Evolution Reveals a Universe without Design* (New York: Norton, 1986), 1.

3. George Gaylord Simpson, "Plan and Purpose in Nature," *Scientific Monthly,* June 1947, 481-95.

4. William Dembski, *The Design Revolution* (Downers Grove, IL: InterVarsity Press, 2004), p. 27.

5. Interview from "Chance or Design," Renewing America's Mind DVD (Dallas: Point of View, 2007).

6. William Dembski, "Still Spinning Just Fine: A Response to Ken Miller" 2.17.03, v. 1, http://www.designinference.com/documents/2003.02.Miller_Response.htm.

7. William Dembski, *The Design Inference: Eliminating Chance Through Small Probabilities* (Cambridge: Cambridge University Press, 1998), 36.

8. Norman Geisler and Frank Turek, *I Don't Have Enough Faith to Be an Atheist* (Wheaton, IL: Crossway Books, 2004).

9. Dembski, *The Design Inference,* 38.

10. Ibid., 3.

11. Carl Sagan, *Contact* (New York: Simon & Schuster, 1985).

12. Stephen Meyer, "Intelligent Design: The Origin of Biological Information and the Higher Taxonomic Categories," *Proceedings of the Biological Society of Washington* 117 (2007), 213-39, http://www.discovery.org/scripts/viewDB/index.php?command=view& id=2177.

13. Nancy Pearcey, "Copying the Human Script: Genome Projects Raises Hopes, Fears," *World,* July 8, 2000.

14. Charles Thaxton, Walter Bradley, and Roger Olsen, *The Mystery of Life's Origin* (New York: Philosophical Library, 1984).

15. David Swift, *Evolution Under the Microscope: A Scientific Critique of the Theory of Evolution* (Stirling University, UK: Leighton Academic, 2002).

16. Franklin Harold, *The Way of the Cell* (Cary, NC: Oxford University Press, 2001), 205.

17. Dean Kenyon and Gary Steinman, *Biochemical Predestination* (NY: McGraw-Hill, 1969).

18. Sir Peter Medawar, "Remarks by the Chairman," in *Mathematical Challenges to the Neo-Darwinian Interpretation of Evolution* (Philadelphia: Wistar Institute Press, 1966, No. 5), xi.

19. Murray Eden, "Inadequacies as a Scientific Theory," in *Mathematical Challenges,* 11.

20. Stanislaw M. Ulam, "How to Formulate Mathematically Problems of Rate of Evolution," in *Mathematical Challenges,* 21.

21. Marcel Schutzenberger, "Algorithms and Neo-Darwinian Theory," in *Mathematical Challenges,* 75.

22. James Shapiro and Richard von Sternberg, "Why Repetitive DNA Is Essential to Genome Function," *Biological Reviews* 80 (2005): 1–24.

23. Roy Britten, "Coding Sequences of Functioning Human Genes Derived Entirely from Mobile Element Sequences," *Proceedings of the National Academy of Sciences* 101 (November 30, 2004): 16825–830.

24. Fazale Rana, "Yet Another Use for 'Junk' DNA," http://www.reasons.org/resources/fff/ 2000issue03/index.shtml#junk_dna.

25. Stephen Gould, *The Panda's Thumb* (New York: Norton, 1980), 20-21.

26. Jay Olshansky, Bruce Carnes, Robert Butler, "If Humans Were Built to Last," *Scientific American,* 284 (March 2001) 70-75.

27. Rich Deem, "Bad Designs in Biology? Why the Best Examples are Bad," www. godandscience.org/evolution/designgonebad.html.

Chapter 6—Intelligent Design in Astronomy

1. Carl Sagan, *Pale Blue Dot* (New York: Ballantine Books, 1994), 7.

2. A discussion of these factors can be found in Stephen Dick, *Life on Other Worlds: The 20th-Century Extraterrestrial Life Debate* (Cambridge: Cambridge University Press, 1998), 209-20.

3. Peter Ward and Donald Brownlee, *Rare Earth: Why Complex Life Is Uncommon in the Universe* (New York: Copernicus, 2000).

4. Gonzalez and Richards, *The Privileged Planet* (Washington, DC: Regnery, 2004), xiii.

5. Interview from "Chance or Design," Renewing America's Mind DVD (Dallas: Point of View, 2007).

6. Dennis Overbye, "Zillions of Universes?" *New York Times,* October 28, 2003.

7. George Greenstein, *The Symbiotic Universe: Life and Mind in the Cosmos* (New York: William Morrow, 1988), 85-90.

8. Paul Davies, "A Brief History of the Multiverse," *New York Times,* April 12, 2003.

9. Gonzalez and Richards, *The Privileged Planet.*

10. Ibid., 11.

11. Interview from "Chance or Design," Renewing America's Mind DVD (Dallas: Point of View, 2007).

12. Ibid.

13. Gonzalez and Richards, *Privileged Planet,* xv.

14. Ibid., 327.

15. Hugh Ross, "Probability for Life on Earth," 2004 April Update, http://www.reasons.org/resources/apologetics/design_evidences/200404_probabilities_for_life_on_earth.shtml.

16. Dr. Hugh Ross, "Where Did the Universe Come From? New Scientific Evidence for the Existence of God," presented in South Barrington, Illinois, April 16, 1994.

17. Fred Hoyle, "The Universe: Some Past and Present Reflections," *Annual Review of Astronomy and Astrophysics,* vol. 20, 1982, 16.

18. Greenstein, *Symbiotic Universe,* 26-27.

19. Ibid., 223.

20. Gregg Easterbrook, "The new convergence," *Wired,* December 2002.

21. Cited in Overbye, "Zillions of Universes?"

22. Heinz Pagels, "A Cozy Cosmology," *The Sciences,* March/April 1985, 35-38.

Chapter 7—Intelligent Design in Biology

1. Michael Behe, *Darwin's Black Box* (New York: Free Press, 1996).

2. Francis Crick, *Life Itself: Its Origins and Nature* (New York: Simon & Schuster, 1981), 70-71.

3. Bruce Alberts, "The Cell as a Collection of Protein Machines," *Cell,* February 6, 1998, 291-94.

4. Behe, *Darwin's Black Box,* 39.

5. Interview from "Chance or Design," Renewing America's Mind DVD (Dallas: Point of View, 2007).

6. Charles Darwin, *On the Origin of Species* (Cambridge: Harvard University Press, 1964), 189.

7. Interview from "Chance or Design," Renewing America's Mind DVD (Dallas: Point of View, 2007).

8. Behe, *Darwin's Black Box,* 72.

9. Ibid., 73.

10. Interview from "Chance or Design," Renewing America's Mind DVD (Dallas: Point of View, 2007).

11. Kenneth Miller, "The Flagellum Unspun: The Collapse of Irreducible Complexity," in William Dembski and Michael Ruse (eds.), *Debating Design: From Darwin to DNA* (Cambridge: Cambridge University Press, 2004), 87.

12. Scott Minnich and Stephen Meyer, "Genetic Analysis of Coordinate Flagellar and Type III Regulatory Circuits," in M.W. Collins and C.A. Brebbia, eds., *Proceedings of the Second International Conference on Design & Nature* (Rhodes, Greece: WIT Press, 2004), 295-304.

13. William Dembski, "Still Spinning Just Fine: A Response to Ken Miller," February 17, 2003, vol. 1, http://www.designinference.com/documents/2003.02.Miller_Response.htm.

14. Michael Behe, "Irreducible Complexity: Obstacle to Darwinian Evolution," in Dembski and Ruse, eds., *Debating Design,* 360.

15. Darwin, *On the Origin of Species,* 189.

16. Charles Darwin, *The Life and Letters of Charles Darwin,* vol. 2, ed., Francis Darwin (New York: Appleton, 1899), 66–67.

17. Behe, *Darwin's Black Box,* 38-39.

18. Interview from "Chance or Design," Renewing America's Mind DVD (Dallas: Point of View, 2007).

19. D.F. Jones, *Genetics in Plant and Animal Improvement* (New York: John Wiley & Sons, 1924), 414.

20. Edward Deevey, "The Reply: Letter from Birman Wood," in *Yale Review* 61 (1967), 631-36.

21. Lane Lester and Raymond Bohlin, *The Natural Limits to Biological Change* (Grand Rapids, MI: Zondervan, 1984), 95.

22. Ibid., 96.

23. Luther Burbank, quoted in Wilbur Hall, *Partner of Nature* (New York: Appleton-Century, 1939), 89-99.

24. Pierre-Paul Grassé, *Evolution of Living Organisms* (New York: Academic Press, 1977), 87.

25. Wallace Arthur, *The Origin of Animal Body Plans* (Cambridge, UK: Cambridge University Press, 1997), 14.

26. Jonathan Wells, *The Politically Incorrect Guide to Darwinism and Intelligent Design* (Washington, DC: Regnery Publishing, 2006), 36.

Chapter 8—Is Intelligent Design Science?

1. Richard Olmstead, "Intelligent Design Not Science," *Seattle Post-Intelligencer,* August 17, 2005, http://seattlepi.nwsource.com/opinion/236793_inteldop.html.

2. Michael Ruse, "Creation Science Is Not Science," *Science, Technology, & Human Values,* vol. 7, no. 40, (Summer 1982), 72-78.

3. Alvin Plantinga, "Whether ID Is Science Isn't Semantics," *Science and Theology News,* March 7, 2006, http://www.stnews.org/Commentary-2690.htm.

4. Thomas Kuhn, *The Structure of Scientific Revolutions* (Chicago: University of Chicago Press, 1962).

5. Posted at http://www.dissentfromdarwin.org/.

6. Richard Dawkins, *The Blind Watchmaker* (New York: Norton, 1986), 6.

7. Daniel Dennett, *Consciousness Explained* (Boston: Back Bay Books, 1991).

8. Peter Singer, *A Darwinian Left: Politics, Evolution, and Cooperation* (New Haven, CT: Yale University Press, 2000), 6.

9. Norman Geisler and Kerby Anderson, *Origin Science* (Grand Rapids: Baker, 1987).

10. Ibid., 15.

11. Ibid., 14.

12. Ibid., 16.

13. Ibid.

14. Interview from "Chance or Design," Renewing America's Mind DVD (Dallas: Point of View, 2007).

15. William Dembski, *No Free Lunch* (Lanham, MD: Rowman & Littlefield, 2002).

16. William Dembski, *Debating Design* (Cambridge: Cambridge University Press, 2004).

17. Michael Behe, *Darwin's Black Box* (New York: Free Press, 1996).

18. Kenneth Miller, *Finding Darwin's God* (New York: Harper, 2000).

19. Ian Musgrave's chapter in Matt Young, *Why Intelligent Design Fails* (Rutgers, NJ: Rutgers, 2004).

20. Keith Lockitch, "The Bait and Switch of Intelligent Design: Religion Masquerading as Science," *Capitalism,* May 3, 2005, http://www.capmag.com/article.asp?ID=4216.

21. "Theologian Says Intelligent Design is Religion," MSNBC, September 30, 2005, http://www.msnbc.msn.com/id/9543398/.

22. Georgia Purdom, "Intelligent Design Movement: Does the Identity of the Creator Really Matter?" *Answers,* May 2, 2006, http://www.answersingenesis.org/articles/am/v1/n1/intelligent-design-movement.

23. Hugh Ross, "More Than Intelligent Design," *Facts for Faith,* Issue 10, http://www.reasons.org/resources/fff/2002issue10/index.shtml#more_than_id.

24. Michael Crichton, "Aliens Cause Global Warming," speech at California Institute of Technology, January 17, 2003, http://www.michaelcrichton.com/speech-alienscauseglobalwarming.html.

Chapter 9—Should Intelligent Design Be Taught in Schools?

1. Phillip Johnson, *Darwin on Trial* (Downers Grove, IL: InterVarsity, 1991), 113-24.

2. Ibid., 114.

3. Ibid., 115.

4. Press release from Dover Area School District, November 19, 2004.

5. David De Wolf, et al., *Traipsing into Evolution: Intelligent Design and the Kitzmiller vs. Dover Decision* (Seattle, WA: Discovery Institute Press, 2006).

6. *Kitzmiller v. Dover,* 400 F. Supp. 2d 707 (M.D. Pa. 2005).

7. Larry Laudan, "The Demise of the Demarcation Problem," in Michael Ruse, ed., *But Is It Science?* (Amherst, MA: Prometheus, 1983), 337-50.

8. Del Ratzch, *Nature, Design, and Science: The Status of Design in Natural Science* (Albany, NY: State University Press, 2001), 147.

9. De Wolf, *Traipsing into Evolution.*

10. Michael Ruse, "Creation Science Is Not Science," *Science, Technology, & Human Values,* vol. 7, no. 40 (Summer 1982), 72-78.

11. Interview from "Chance or Design," Renewing America's Mind DVD (Dallas: Point of View, 2007).

12. Alvin Plantinga, "Whether ID Is Science Isn't Semantics," *Science and Theology News,* March 7, 2006, http://www.stnews.org/Commentary-2690.htm.

13. Consider the scientists who sign the statement "A Scientific Dissent from Darwinism," http://www.dissentfromdarwin.org/. This list of signatures continues to grow every year.

14. De Wolf, *Traipsing into Evolution,* 22.

15. "Famous Atheist Now Believes in God," December 9, 2004, ABC News.

16. Gary Habermas, "Atheist Becomes Theist," *Philosophi Christi* (Winter 2004), http://www.biola.edu/antonyflew.

17. Claudia Wallis, "The Evolution Wars," *Time,* August 7, 2005, http://www.time.com/time/printout/0,8816,1090909,00.html.

18. Mark Bergin, "Teach the Controversy," *World,* July 21, 2007, 14.

19. Stephen Meyer, et al., *Explore Evolution: The Arguments for and Against Neo-Darwinism* (Melbourne: Hill House Publishers, 2007).

20. Ibid.

21. Ric Anderson, "Critics: E-mail Reveals Intent," *Topeka Capital-Journal,* November 24, 2005, 10A.

22. Jonathan Wells, *Icons of Evolution* (Washington, DC: Regnery, 2000), 193.

23. Ibid., 58.

24. Mark Bergin, "Publish and Perish," *World,* May 26, 2007, 24.

25. Ibid.

26. Statement on Intelligent Design by Iowa State University Faculty, http://www.biology.iastate.edu/STATEMENT.htm.

27. Mark Bergin, "Crisis Averted," *World,* August 25, 2007, 21.

28. Mark Bergin, "Not So Fast," *World,* September 15, 2007, 34.

29. Ibid.

30. Accessed at http://www.baylor.edu/character/index.php?id=13027.

Chapter 10—Origins and the Bible

1. Guillermo Gonzalez and Jay W. Richards. *The Privileged Planet: How Our Place in the Cosmos Is Designed for Discovery* (Washington, DC: Regnery Publishing, 2004).

2. Interview from "Chance or Design," Renewing America's Mind DVD (Dallas: Point of View, 2007).

3. Michael Behe, *Darwin's Black Box: The Biochemical Challenge to Evolution* (New York: Free Press, 1996).

4. Editorial board, "An Atheist's Apostasy," *Dallas Morning News,* December 15, 2004.

5. J.P. Moreland and John Mark Reynolds, *Three Views of Creation and Evolution* (Grand Rapids: Zondervan, 1999).

6. Henry Morris, *The Genesis Record* (Grand Rapids: Baker, 1976), 37-81.

7. Everett Koop and Francis Schaeffer, *Whatever Happened to the Human Race* (Westchester, IL: Crossway Books, 1983), 112.

8. Hugh Ross, *Creation and Time* (Colorado Springs: NavPress, 1994), 45-72.

9. The Clergy Letter Project, http://www.butler.edu/clergyproject/rel_evol_sun2007.htm.

10. Howard Van Till, et al., *Portraits of Creation* (Grand Rapids: Eerdmans, 1990), 232-42.

11. Francis Schaeffer, *No Final Conflict* (Downers Grove, IL: InterVarsity, 1975).

12. Francis Collins, "Can You Believe in God and Evolution?" *Time,* August 7, 2005, http://www.time.com/time/magazine/article/0,9171,1090921,00.html.

13. Schaeffer, *No Final Conflict,* 24.

Other Harvest House Books
by Kerby Anderson

HOMOSEXUALITY
A sensitive and factual survey of a difficult topic, this book addresses the essentials you need to know about controversial issues such as the causes of homosexuality, the legalization of same-sex marriages, popular myths about homosexuality, and whether it's possible for homosexuals to change.

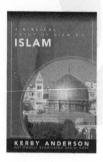

ISLAM
Do Christians and Muslims worship the same God? Is Islam a religion of peace? Does the Qur'an support the martyrdom of suicide bombers? How do the Bible and the Qur'an contradict each other? What is the extent of the threat from radical Islam? These questions and more are answered from a biblical perspective.

HARVEST HOUSE
PUBLISHERS